THE TRUTH ABOUT ILLNESS, UNHAPPINESS AND STRESS?

Barry & Winnie
Durdant-Hollamby

New edition

THE ART
of
CHANGE

First Published in the United Kingdom by:
The Art of Change
PO Box 441
East Grinstead
West Sussex RH18 5DH
www.artofchange.co.uk
email: welcome@artofchange.co.uk

ISBN 09530063-1-X
978 0 953 0063 1 1

All case studies in this book are based on real experiences. Names and personal details have been changed.

Grateful acknowledgement is made to the publishers and authors of all the books from which quotes have been used.

Typeset and cover lay-out:
David Brown, Maynards Green, Heathfield, Sussex TN21 0DG.

Cover photograph:
Dianne McFadden

Additional proof-reading:
Margaret Durdant-Hollamby
Anna Durdant-Hollamby

Special thanks to Wendy Brown

Printing and binding:
Lightning Source Uk Ltd.
www.lightningsource.com

Contents

For Alexander 'Sasha' Slepov

Foreword

Here you are then. A book in your hands entitled *The Truth about Illness, Unhappiness and Stress?* A key to the book is in the question mark.

This book does not give you any answers or quick fixes. It does not promise to reveal the truth. Quite the opposite.

It gets you asking questions that will lead you to your own perfect answers.

This book is inspirational, stimulating, even challenging. It clearly introduces you to a world of possibilities while questioning many long-held, traditional understandings about health and life.

Whatever your background, life issue, state of health, beliefs or mindset – and whether you can or cannot explain the reason for holding this book in your hands at this moment – do read through it carefully. If you don't you may well miss something that could just change your life for the better.

The concepts are fully supported by case studies. The authors share experiences that span a wide spectrum of life and health issues including cancer, depression, addiction, financial loss, relationships and dying.

All those people who were willing to change have found that these ideas have helped them to find the courage, clarity and inspiration to embrace changes that at first may have seemed unimaginable. Reading the case studies alone brings inspiration to look outside your comfort zone of knowledge and accepted "truth".

Practical tools are introduced – all of which the authors use to help clients daily – with research information and ideas from ancient and modern fields of well-being to support their effectiveness. At the end of each chapter there is a checklist to help you to integrate the concepts presented into your life.

Covering health, children, relationships, money and death, *The Truth about Illness, Unhappiness and Stress?* is comprehensive in its invitation to you to explore your own life situation.

I can speak as someone who has embraced these ideas and who, with careful, patient and loving support from the authors over the last 10 years, has changed her own life dramatically. I feel privileged to have worked through my own illness, unhappiness and stress with their unique approaches to life.

Having come from a business background with a science degree and a place of traditional, scientific viewpoints on health, today I hold a very different and empowering perspective on life and my part within it.

Not so long ago I readily put what I do now in the 'weird and wacky' camp. I was also experiencing illness, unhappiness and stress in abundance. However my own questioning and the exploration of the concepts which the authors present in this book, challenged my view of the truth. I was taken right out of my comfort zone. What I ended up creating was a life of greater health, happiness and abundance during which time I have become a fully qualified vibrational medicine consultant and researcher.

I came to them for help and now find myself helping others too.

You can choose the easy option of staying in your comfort zone, or rise to the challenge and explore the great outside. The choice is yours. Remember, the common view once held was that the world was flat...

Shelley Sishton BSC Hons,
Dip.Vib.Med (IFVM), ITEC.
www.purelyessences.com
www.the-energy-centre.com

Introduction

This book is an invitation. An invitation to you to consider a very different understanding of the nature of illness, unhappiness and stress.

All of these are usually thought of as states or conditions that are not wanted. They are misfortunes that strike at random, are beyond control and have no meaning.

Or are they?

Illness, unhappiness and stress – or dis-ease as all of these will be called in this book – may in fact be signs on a surface level that something has become unbalanced at a deeper emotional level. It is whether we choose to consider this possibility and how we then elect to deal with these signs that we believe holds the key to present and future good health and happiness.

We believe that good health and not dis-ease is the natural state of the human being. Most of us are, after all, born with perfect health. Dis-ease is something that we acquire without realising how at various times throughout life. We may each have the ability to reduce our suffering or in some cases even rid ourselves entirely of dis-ease. Perhaps it is just a question of knowing how. This book is our invitation to find out some of the simple truths and ideas that may lead to better health and a happier life.

There is one very important point to remember all the way through this book. PLEASE DO NOT BELIEVE A WORD WE SAY!

All we ask is that you retain an open mind. Let your own feelings and experiences then tell you what works for you and what does not. We are not out to prove anything – we are here to get you thinking outside the box. We would love you to challenge any limiting or erroneous conditioning and belief systems you may have if it feels appropriate to do so.

We would like to make it clear that we are not against orthodox medicine nor opposed to the caring work carried out by nurses, doctors and consultants the world over. If anything we are trying to make their work easier by helping you, the patient, to do everything you possibly can to create 'self-health', thus reducing your dependency upon health carers of any sort.

You can help to create self-health in many ways. There are many subjects that we do not cover in this book that are of great significance. One of the most important areas in which to increase your self-knowledge is that of nutrition. What you put into your body needs to be as pure and unprocessed as possible. If you feel you would benefit from expert guidance on this subject please refer to the recommended reading at the end of this book or do some research to discover some of the ground-breaking information that is widely available.

We would also ask you to remember this; we are not asking you to give us your time, we are asking you to give yourself the time. Be patient, be thorough and you may witness improvements in your life. Improvements that **you** will have made happen. Be prepared to learn, be prepared to change and do not try to hurry anything. There is no need.

Please also bear in mind that whatever your current state of health there is one life ingredient that is guaranteed to make you feel better. Never underestimate the healing power of laughter.

4

1

Five Modern Myths

"We cannot solve life's problems except by solving them."
M Scott Peck,
The Road Less Travelled

We're going to start by looking at what it really means to take responsibility for yourself. Let's begin by taking a look at five contemporary myths that in our experience are believed by many people.

Myth 1 – I Am A Busy Person Therefore I Am A Responsible Person

We tend to measure responsibility in various ways: for example, house ownership, employment, voluntary work or creating a family. We say that by nature of the fact that "I am a director of my own company", or "I am a parent of three children and hold down a paid job too", or "I am a dedicated nurse working long and unsocial hours" – we are being responsible people and therefore must be taking responsibility for ourselves.

This is not necessarily true. Being a responsible person and taking full responsibility for yourself can be two very different things. Doing anything that causes you dis-ease – whatever the reason and whatever the dis-ease – may be entirely due to your own misunderstanding of what it means to take complete responsibility for yourself.

PHIL

Phil got up at 5.30 every morning to catch the 6.15 train to work. He generally worked through until 6.00pm and would return home by about 8.30 most nights. Being a caring young dad and a committed employee, he found himself hurrying in both directions to fulfil his obligations; train delays and cancellations were often the cause of great stress.

It wasn't long before he started to suffer from stress and anxiety. Being in that daily state of low-grade panic is debilitating to even the strongest of constitutions. But Phil felt he had to keep up the

pattern in order to sustain the happiness of the family and keep his job.

And yet the happiness of his family was already negatively affected because the demands of Phil's job deprived them of much of his emotional support, his company and his friendship. His partner and children accepted his moods and his stress as inevitable and developed coping strategies. But the stress grew and his effectiveness at work was compromised. This didn't go unnoticed by his employers and Phil found himself having to justify his performance on a weekly basis, all of which added significantly to his stress.

So, even whilst he was enjoying the house, the car and the holidays, Phil was also suffering from the stress of supporting such a big house, such a nice car and such expensive holidays. Believing these items to be integral to the happiness of his family, he had started to live under the illusion that his personal suffering was unavoidable. And if the family had looked around them and observed their friends and neighbours they would probably have seen most other people in similar situations and would therefore have accepted that this was how

life had to be.

As Phil's stress mounted however, his health problems became increasingly hard to ignore. But instead of paying attention to the ever louder protests from his body or stopping to ask himself or his family what any of them really wanted, he continued his lifestyle unchanged, in the belief that he was doing the best thing for everyone. The result for Phil was the loss of his job and short-term health, something that finally forced him and his family to reassess their priorities in life.

It may be in this simple misunderstanding of the true meaning of responsibility that Phil's dis-ease lay. He was doing what he thought was the responsible thing to do, but he was not living in a way that was in his, or his family's, long-term interests. His health could only continue to fail as long as he continued this apparently 'responsible' yet stressful life.

Myth 2 – In Life Dis-ease Is Inevitable

This is probably a good time to remind you of something that we said in the introduction – remember the bit about not believing a word we say?

This is where we need you to be open to a new possibility – don't believe us, just be open, just a little bit, to the radical idea that somehow we may not all have to look forward to periods of dis-ease after all.

A Message From The Body

It is the authors' belief that when we suffer dis-ease it is a sign to tell us that something deeper than just our physical body is out of balance. This sign may come in many different forms; it may be like a big red stop light that forces us to drop everything. Examples of this might include heart disease, cancer, major depression or pneumonia. Or it may be as a small beacon flashing intermittently in the distance in the form of less serious but recurring illness such as repeated bouts of minor depression, colds, allergies, indigestion, migraines, or even a proneness to accidents. Although relatively minor now, if there is a deeper cause which is left unresolved, it is possible that more serious dis-ease will follow.

Dis-ease Is Not Inevitable

So how about this for a radical thought: dis-ease is neither random nor inevitable. Howls of outrage and disbelief? Well, we told you it was a radical thought. But maybe we all play some part in the way that disease develops in our bodies and minds. Furthermore, if this is true, could it mean that there is a way to lessen our suffering?

It could be that we are not meant to live any part of our lives in this unnatural state. Maybe the reason we do get dis-ease is because our internal guidance system is trying to get a message to us about our lives and sometimes the only way it can do this is to resort to physical distress. Dis-ease could mean that something in our life is, or has been, out of harmony with our true needs.

Myth 3 – Other People Cure Us

"WHAT"! we hear you cry. "But what about doctors and surgeons and healers and operations and drugs and all that stuff? Operations are successful and people are fixed. By others. How can you say that it's a myth that other people cure us?"

Just bear with us a minute (and that includes all you doctors, therapists and healers) – provided you haven't already thrown the book in the bin. Here's our take on 'curing' other people.

Is All Healing Ultimately Self-Healing?

It is our suggestion that no one has ever been completely cured by a doctor, therapist, healer or any other form of outside helper. By 'completely' we mean in mind, body and spirit. We believe that the only person who can fully heal us is ourself. This is not to say that a visit to a doctor or healer cannot be beneficial in bringing about a physical improvement; but it is to suggest that such outside intervention may only be a tool that we use along the way to complete self-healing.

Returning briefly to the first myth about responsibility; we would all benefit from erasing the belief that a visit to the doctor means that we are taking responsibility for our health. It is not fair on the medical profession and it is not fair on any one of us. All we do by going for medical help before investigating the possibility that maybe we can do something to correct the imbalance ourselves, is hand the responsibility to the doctor. We say to ourselves "I'm alright now, the doctor's given me a prescription or a referral or an injection." And in that same moment we have handed over our responsibility to get better to someone else. We have not stopped to consider where the imbalance may have come from or what we could do to correct it and consequently our own power to heal from within may have been thwarted.

It is of course true that doctors can prescribe drugs to ease symptoms and halt infection, or they can cut out parts of the body where dis-ease has run amok. But is this really a cure? In terms of dis-ease it may be little more than a delaying tactic. Advocates of modern medicine (and, we repeat, we fully acknowledge the valuable role that the skills and devotion of medical professionals can play in our lives) may point to the people who, following medical treatment, have gone on to lead long and happy lives. Understandably these people are proclaimed as 'medical' successes. Could it be however that these people have also played a part in bringing about their own eventual happiness, their own eventual good health? Could it be that they enhanced the effects of the medical treatment that they received?

Addressing The Cause

How might they have done this? Could they have done it by consciously (or subconsciously) making the changes in their lives that addressed the original causes of the dis-ease? The medical intervention may have 'kick-started' this process, ridding them of infection or eradicating pain, but it is possible that these individuals then either knowingly or unknowingly addressed the very elements in their lives that were causing the problem. Medicine may have been no more and no less than a tool that they used to their own best advantage.

The world is moving so fast now and our demand for an instant cure has gathered momentum. The usual response to feeling a symptom growing inside us is to go into 'fix' mode, immediately taking some action that we hope will halt the development of this symptom so we can get on with our busy lives. Would we benefit more from taking time out to rest and reflect on what the symptom may be trying to tell us?

Myth 4 – Illness Is Generally Due To Bad Luck

Ah, the old 'bad luck' chestnut. We're going to let rip with another challenging concept now so here goes....

It's quite normal and understandable to look for someone or something else to blame for the fact that you've become ill, unhappy or stressed. How many times have we all talked about bad luck in relation to illness?

How often do you find people consoling you on your run of bad luck with colds, relationships, poverty or whatever? Somehow blaming your condition on bad luck seems to make it more acceptable and also brings the sympathy that you think will help you to feel better.

No Such Thing As Luck

Well we're going to ask you to stop right there with that old paradigm thinking. We believe that it can be erroneous to blame our conditions on bad luck. Yup, just plain wrong. We're not even convinced (now this really is radical but then you don't have to believe a word we say) that there is any such thing as luck – good or bad.

Let's look at some theoretical but not unusual examples. A woman is diagnosed with cancer. She follows a regimen of treatment and some time later is pronounced completely clear of cancer. Is it really due to bad luck if she goes on to develop cancer again?

Is it really due to bad luck that the young child whose ear infection has been suppressed with antibiotics goes on to suffer repeated bouts of ear trouble? Is it really due to bad luck that the person who experiences problems in a relationship goes on to experience similar problems in other relationships?

Like most people you probably tend to interpret these events, quite understandably, as bad luck. It is at this point that you make yourself a victim of misfortune. After all if you're not a victim then that might mean you have some responsibility for your negative state of being. And if you are responsible then that would imply that you have failed to avoid these negative experiences and are no good at this whole life thing – and that could make you feel even more depressed. And besides which – why, oh why, would you ever want to create pain or suffering for yourself anyway?

Before you go into a state of blind panic or red rage please read on.

Whatever your state of dis-ease, whether work-induced stress, medical side-effects or any other form of illness or unhappiness, isn't it possible that you have played a part in creating that state? This is not about apportioning blame, it is about claiming back your power. You've chosen your work, you've chosen your relationships, you've chosen every aspect of your life as it exists at present. You may therefore also be responsible for whatever mental and physical symptoms these aspects of life have brought into existence – even though this creation was unconscious. Obviously you didn't mean to do this and it is a really bad idea to start blaming yourself for doing so at any stage. But it is worth considering the possibility that bad luck has played no part in this process.

MICHELLE

Michelle had brought up three children single-handedly for many years . She had knocked herself out to provide for them in every way possible. She prepared their packed lunches and delivered each child individually to school prior to going on to work herself. She went without a lunch hour to enable herself to leave work early to return home and prepare their evening meals and see to the other domestic chores. She worried incessantly about their health, often booking doctor's appointments at the onset of childhood illnesses such as chicken pox, German measles and even heavy colds or flu.

As the children grew up their needs naturally increased. Being used to a mum who sorted everything out for them they continued to have this expectation. She found herself frequently having to chase her children to keep up to date with their studies and often having to send letters of excuse to the school for uncompleted home-work; she received few offers of help from them around the house, either preparing meals, washing or keeping the place tidy and she often had to work through their assignments with them showing them how to get a decent mark. She had no social life outside of her children.

By the time the oldest son went on to university, Michelle was mentally and physically exhausted and the young man was completely incapable of looking after himself. After a couple of months of partying he went into a steep depression when faced with the reality that he had virtually no tools to cope with living. Washing, eating, financial planning, deadlines, research – he was impotent to do any of it. He just had no idea how and found himself faced with huge debts, a filthy room and a mounting pile of unfinished and overdue essays.

Faced with such stress the young man left university and returned home putting even more pressure on the mother. She now had to cope with her own weakening physical and mental state and a depressed oldest son. This combination impacted negatively on the family as a whole, as rows and stress became the norm and happiness became a rare commodity. Michelle could not believe the appalling luck that had dogged her throughout life.

It wasn't until several years later, by which time Michelle had developed ME and the children had been forced to learn to cope for themselves, that she went through a process of personal change that helped her to see how she had created her own 'luck'. She had thought she had been acting responsibly – giving the children what they needed all the way along the line – but in fact she had been disempowering them by taking their decisions and almost living their lives for them. And in so doing the one person who had needed to remain strong and clear had ended up exhausted and demoralised.

Myth 5 – We Cannot Be Responsible For The 'Bad' Things That Happen To Us Because We Did Not Want Them

Still with us? Okay, try this extension of the above

section on so-called bad luck.

However honest you may think you are with yourself, accepting that you are entirely responsible for the 'bad' or unwanted things that happen to you is a very difficult notion to swallow. It's challenging to contemplate the possibility that you've created or attracted a situation into your life that is wholly undesirable such as illness, unhappiness or stress. Obviously, you didn't want that to happen. As children we have not been taught to accept total responsibility for everything that enters our lives, and nor were our parents or even their parents. And yet we are suggesting that everyone is responsible for creating – albeit unconsciously – whatever their present circumstances may be. People often reject this concept on the basis that it brings about guilt and self-blame to heap on top of the suffering that is already present. But there is no blame to attach to anyone for this – least of all to yourself.

Culture Of Blame And Quick Fix

We have been brought up in a society where blaming someone or something for any undesirable experience is the norm. After blaming misfortune for our ailments we may move on for instance to blaming doctors for the side-effects of particular treatments or for their failure to stop serious conditions from recurring.

But is it any doctor's fault that he/she will only be dealing with symptoms, not causes? Aren't those frequently experienced disadvantages of orthodox medicine – side-effects and lack of long-term cures – products of our own desire to get as quick a fix as possible for whatever ails us in order that we can get back to whatever we are doing? We haven't been taught to recognise dis-ease in whatever shape or form it might manifest as a message to stop our busy-ness. Nor are many of us aware that dis-ease can present a great opportunity to take stock and see where the imbalance might have come from.

The following chapters will indicate further how these myths may play such a central role in our life. It is in the recognition that these established beliefs might be just plain wrong that our real strength may lie.

Checklist

1 Are you being kind to yourself or are you pushing yourself to fulfil commitments every day that you are struggling to meet? Is your life really that of a

responsible person (remember you're not much use to anyone if you become sidelined by serious illness/stress)?

2 It could be that dis-ease is neither random nor inevitable. Are you listening closely enough to your present moment needs for balance and peace?

3 Help your doctors and therapists to be even more effective and give their treatments the best chance of success by taking real and complete responsibility for your own state of being. Take charge of your life!

4 If you are experiencing physical, emotional or mental suffering, take a look at your life right now and try to identify where you may be fuelling the fire of dis-ease.

5 Consider eradicating the words 'bad luck' and 'blame' from your vocabulary!

2

A Quantum Leap

"... frequently our innate sense of what is best for us is short-circuited by suspicion while the intellect, which has never known much about our real needs, decides what to do."

Jean Liedloff,
The Continuum Concept

So far we've talked about the importance of taking responsibility for the state we're in. Now that you've maybe considered taking that responsibility, the next step is to understand how you can help to instigate the conscious decision-making process that might take you a little closer to some of the potential causes of dis-ease.

Quite often complementary therapies work on the basis of a 'preventative' approach. Ideally we would all love to wise up on creating a preventative approach before we are brought to our knees by illness – but how do we do it?

The Purely Physical Approach

Let's take a quick look at where we may have come a little off the rails in the way that we as a society have been encouraged to approach health and illness. Remember the example in Chapter 1 of the woman who has had every cancerous cell removed from her body? Physically she is now entirely free from cancer. There is no physical reason why she should get cancer again. But she has a high chance of doing so statistically. Why?

Or again looking at cancer, surely if a purely physical approach to treatment really is the answer, then cancers of the same type would all respond in the same way to the same treatment. But this doesn't happen.

EMILY & SONIA

By the time Emily and Sonia met for the first time in the women's wing of a cancer hospital, Emily was already a week into her treatment. They came from

very different backgrounds and yet had been brought together by exactly the same type of disease. Emily, who was carrying out her own holistic approach alongside her orthodox treatment, seemed to be making good progress using a new cocktail of cancer-killing chemicals that her consultant had just authorised.

As her progress improved and tests showed a significant reduction in her cancer, the consultant recommended that Sonia, who was suffering from the same cancer, should have the same treatment. Emily's recovery continued. Sonia however did not respond at all.

What medicine finds is that patients with the same diagnosis respond in unique ways to their treatments. A chemotherapy cocktail will invariably have different results on two people with the same cancer. Why should this be so? Is it because there is a deeper cause that is not being dealt with?

Is it possible that many modern treatments may be dealing with the symptoms of an illness – and the physical parts identified as having gone wrong – but that somewhere else there is also an emotional or non-physical driver that in some cases continues to churn out a self-destructive message? Are we, in these cases where the treatment is not ultimately successful, dealing with symptoms but failing somehow to identify causes?

Heresy – Or Thinking Outside The Box

This is powerful stuff and for doctors, nurses, therapists and patients alike what we're saying here could be interpreted as heresy. But please remember, we're not trying to upset anyone, we're trying to get people thinking outside of the traditional box when it comes to health, happiness and well-being. Society has to keep exploring new possibilities in health because we don't yet have all the fixes for cancer, stress, depression and other mental and physical illnesses. Maybe we need to look at our understanding of them in a 'wholistic' way in order to get closer to preventing them and healing them. For prevention ultimately reduces the need for cures at all. Even slight improvements in our prevention rates could slash the nation's health costs.

Physical Causes. Example – Cancer

So let's look at some current theories on some potential causes of cancer. It could be very reasonably argued for instance that the reason a person develops cancer is because they smoked heavily, or were exposed to asbestos in their youth, or were sunburnt too many times – there are many identified physical causes. And yes of course these could certainly be contributory factors in the case of illness. Barry's father for instance was a heavy smoker of non-tipped cigarettes and died of emphysema in his early 60s after a long and difficult illness. There is little doubt that there is a connection between the illness and his smoking.

But what about those people who are exposed to many of the same risks mentioned above but who do not go on to develop the predicted disease?

WINNIE'S GRANDMOTHER

My grandmother smoked at least twenty cigarettes a day from the age of sixteen, and lived to the age of ninety-five, enjoying excellent health until she passed away in her sleep. Oh, and she also liked to have a drink or two every night...

Winnie's granny should logically have developed a lung disease earlier in her life but she didn't. Similarly, not everyone who experiences repeated and severe sunburn will go on to develop skin cancer. Neither will everyone exposed to asbestos particles go on to develop lung cancer. Yet if these carcinogenic influences are so very dangerous and if there are only physical reasons why we become ill – why are there any exceptions, even one?

It is suggested of course that some people are more disposed than others to develop cancer due to their inherited genetic make-up. Whilst this 'cancer gene' theory may also be a contributory factor we do not believe that it can ever be the sole reason for someone to develop cancer – for the same reasons as stated above. Science cannot predict with 100% accuracy which members of a family will develop certain conditions. There must be something else going on as well.

We believe that the answer to our question may lie in understanding a little more about the journey that cancer – or any other form of dis-ease – takes from conception to physical manifestation.

Quantum Physics

The world of quantum physics may seem like a strange place to go for this understanding but in fact Einstein was one of the first people to give the world a scientific explanation of the true nature of physical matter. In simple terms his Theory of Relativity $(e = mc^2)$ states that all matter (i.e. rocks, trees, people, water, buildings, planets etc) is in fact vibrating energy.

What are the implications of this statement in relation to our health?

Ancient Wisdom

Before we attempt to shed any light on this question, it is worth noting that the ancient systems of healing from across the world – in China, India, Australia and the Americas for example – based their healing ideas on this concept of energy. They gave birth to systems such as acupuncture and vibrational medicine (flower essences, homeopathy, energy healing) that were entirely based upon the existence of flows of energy. For thousands of years, long before Einstein's Theory of Relativity overturned Isaac Newton's theories, many people have known instinctively that there is more to the human body than the solid physical form we can all see and touch.

This ancient knowledge concurs with Einstein's theories in the understanding that the body is just energy vibrating at a certain frequency, and our thoughts and emotions are also energy vibrating at a different frequency – higher than that of the physical body. The higher frequencies cannot be seen with the physical eyes – though many healers, shamans and 'sensitives' claim to see or feel some of these energy fields, which exist both inside and outside the physical body. (The concept of matter energy responding to thought energy has been ratified by scientists carrying out advanced quantum experiments where they have found that the thoughts of the 'observer' in an experiment impact upon the interaction and behaviour of the particles. Literally, mind over matter.)

Energy Body

You what? An energy body? Sounds a bit Star Trekky doesn't it? Let's see if we can give you some real proof here…

Sorry, no we can't. You have our permission to throw the book away again and get your money back.

You see technology has not yet developed foolproof means of recording or observing the 'energy body or counterpart' in order to prove its existence scientifically.

However, it's probably worth bearing in mind that holistic practitioners all over the world continue to draw on this ancient wisdom and focus their healing techniques on the body's subtle energies, with or without scientific proof, on the basis that the daily results experienced by their patients are all the evidence they need that such energy exists. Are they really all bonkers – patients and practitioners alike – or is there something going on here?

And, if this energy body or counterpart does exist, what does it do and how might it affect dis-ease?

Gossip and speculation time. And we love a bit of that.

It is possible that the energy body provides the life-force that drives the physical body. But remember, you may not want to believe that bit. Or the bit that follows…

When the physical body begins to show signs of dis-ease, could it be because there has already been damage at this subtler energy level?

If this energy body does exist then being non-physical it seems logical that the purely physical effects of things such as toxins, bacteria, viruses, drugs or even violent trauma cannot harm it – directly. It seems plausible, if totally radical, to assume that the only one thing that could damage something made up of energy would be a greater amount of negative energy. And if we stop for a minute to identify how negative energy impacts in our daily lives, we come to ground in one place. Stress.

Negative Energy = Stress

Stress, stress, stress, stress. It's just another word for negative energy. It's everywhere and it takes many forms. You may experience it as unreleased emotions such as grief, bereavement, worry, fear, guilt, frustration, jealousy, anger, or anxiety. You may experience it as the shock waves resulting from a physical trauma such as surgery, a car crash, overworking, substance abuse, or pollution in our environment. Whichever of these or other examples of stress is the cause of our particular dis-ease, the point is that a breakdown may have been caused at the energy level we've spoken about and at this moment dis-ease may have been born.

TERRI

In the 18 months prior to our first meeting, media representative Terri had missed 6 months of work due to repeated bouts of different illnesses. She suffered badly with colds and flu, was clearly stressed and very susceptible to viruses.

We taught her basic relaxation methods, how to listen to her body and how better to balance her time. We also taught her how to express her truth more clearly. In the 18 months since we started working with her she has had no more than a handful of days off work, she has been promoted and she feels much more in control of her life and her body. And yet we did nothing physical and gave her nothing physical.

Indulge us a bit more whilst we probe further. Imagine that we have got an energy body and that our energy body is like a suit of armour that protects our physical body. All the time that our suit of armour is maintained in perfect order, our physical and mental health remains good. But when the protective armour is damaged, the physical body becomes prone to attack from outside until the armour itself has been repaired.

Maybe in this very simple analogy we are beginning to see how the physical symptom, which modern medicine often treats as the problem, is in fact possibly the last stage of a breakdown in energy which may well have started at a much earlier time – sometimes as far back as in the womb.

It is of course true that when dis-ease has reached this late stage, the physical symptom needs to be addressed, but correcting it alone seems unlikely to prevent another attacking element breaching the same hole in the armour. This perhaps is why some people seem to be permanently in a state of dis-ease. Their energy body has been damaged and they are unable to fend off attacking forces.

But for those whose armour remains intact, whose energy body has not been damaged by stress, virtually nothing can pose a threat to their physical body. This could be the reason why some people can be exposed to supposedly lethal forces and yet suffer no illness.

This explanation also might give us an understanding of how a person 'miraculously' recovers from an illness that has been diagnosed as terminal and untreatable. They have somehow reached the root cause of their stress and altered their circumstances in order to eradicate it, possibly effecting a complete repair at the energy level, leading to a recovery at the physical level against all expectations.

How? Let's take a look at the role our emotions play in all this.

Significance Of Emotions

Emotions, which we believe act like an 'inner guidance system', may be designed to provide you with every bit of help that you could ever possibly need in life. They could hold the key to your own abilities to heal. If you're struggling with this concept you might want to consider the word 'intuition' and its literal meaning – tuition or teaching from within. Other than believing in the existence of this benign internal wisdom, your next biggest challenge lies in trying to recognise what on earth these emotions are trying to communicate to you.

Trusting Intuition

Everyone has at some point been aware of having this guidance; you might for example have experienced it as the gut feeling of knowing that a house you had just walked into was 'the one for you' even though you may have had at that point little intellectual information about the suitability of the house; you may have experienced it as a 'mother's intuition' regarding the well-being of your baby or child. Sometimes people call this guidance intuition, sometimes instinct, sometimes emotion, hunch or gut feeling. The question is, if this really is something you can trust how can you become better at recognising it?

Once you have made the decision to take responsibility for yourself, you may start to take notice of your own internal signals in a way that you would not if another person were in charge of your healing. You'll begin to find that you can become aware of the dangers of dis-ease earlier – there are many warning signs that we customarily ignore – and you will also find that there is much you can do using natural methods to prevent the manifestation of illness or to heal it once it has taken hold.

It is the focusing of attention in the wrong place

that may be preventing the recognition of internal warnings. We have not been brought up to 'listen' to ourselves and so we don't look for meaning in illness. We carry on with our lives in exactly the same manner, hoping that these uncomfortable moments will somehow disappear. But they do not. And they will not. It is our belief that it is only when you cease shifting the responsibility for your well-being to someone else that you can regain your ability to provide yourself with a life free from suffering.

SUSAN

Susan had been diagnosed with stomach cancer and had been receiving medical treatment for it for several months prior to pursuing a more holistic approach. Up until she decided to take a more active role in her own healing, the treatment she had been receiving had failed to have any positive impact on her cancer and she was at a very low ebb both mentally and physically.

We met up and chatted about subjects such as the present moment, meditation, relaxation, quantum physics, support networks and the concept of taking responsibility for one's own well-being. She felt empowered by these ideas and she also felt she had nothing to lose by adopting this different approach. So she started taking her own involvement in her health much more seriously – up to now she had just been handing a broken machine over to the mechanics to fix.

Susan immediately started to feel more confident about her situation. Several weeks after she had stepped up her own role in her health she received her first major piece of encouragement since she had first been diagnosed – scan results indicated that she had gone into 'remission' status. But that wasn't the end of the cancer.

In the following two years her illness returned twice – and interestingly in the period leading up to each new diagnosis, Susan had allowed the pressures and stresses of life to start bossing her around again. But on both occasions Susan found herself able to dig a little deeper into her own resources to help overcome the illness. She kept up her orthodox medical treatment and alongside this she introduced a combination of complementary therapies and self-help techniques.

Susan was drawn to these approaches initially

through blind panic because orthodox medicine was not producing the results she wanted. It is interesting to note that her treatments only seemed to become really effective when she became more involved in her own health. Now she knows herself and her own capabilities far better. Her fear of her own body letting her down is today vastly reduced – she listens to herself much more and no longer drives herself in the way that she used to. She has learnt that her own happiness and peace of mind are vital ingredients in maintaining her health. She has also witnessed how, when she has ignored her own needs and allowed more stress back into her life, her illness has invariably resurfaced – even though the medical treatment has continued throughout.

Eight years ago Susan knew nothing of the power of the individual. Today she lives more for the moment, considers herself a better mother and wife and is able to say that her illness has been a process through which she has now managed to learn much about life (even if it is a process she would not care to repeat). Overall, cancer has been a teacher that has helped her find greater happiness. She has been in remission for over seven years at the time of writing.

Of course everyone wants to know what cured the illness. No one will ever know for sure. Was it one thing alone? Was it a combination of different factors? Whilst we can't claim that taking more responsibility for herself was in itself a cure, we would suggest that it might have been a contributory factor – perhaps even a crucial factor – in enabling everything Susan was doing to bring about her healing.

Not Rejecting Medical Help

We need to make an important point at this stage about working on your health with or without third-party help. For those of you who feel threatened by the thought of casting outside intervention to one side, please note that we are suggesting no such thing. Taking responsibility for your own health doesn't have to mean turning your back entirely upon the medical profession or anything else. People who have been on heavy doses of steroids, anti-depressants or other drugs for instance, and who suddenly stop taking them can suffer serious side effects. We are not advocating that people suddenly become independent to the degree of foolhardiness.

Neither are we saying that medicine, be it

orthodox, complementary or alternative, isn't able to act as the catalyst by which someone may begin this natural process of true healing. But we are advocating that you must understand the consequences of every drug or treatment that you are prescribed, and that you must research what side effects as well as benefits these treatments may produce. You need to understand fully what part any medical treatment or complementary therapy will play in your journey to reaching the cause of the dis-ease before you agree to have it. For the aim has to be to reach the cause.

The Russian Doll

Imagine a child playing with a Russian doll and her goal is to reach the smallest doll in the middle. If the child uses a hammer, the destination is unlikely to be reached without all the outer dolls becoming damaged, possibly beyond repair. But ask the child to use her fingers, her own natural methods, and sooner or later she will arrive at the centre with all the dolls still unbroken. The journey to the doll in the middle may be slow, frustrating and at times even upsetting, but if the child has the patience to carry on then the goal will be reached.

41

If we could all apply this approach to our own health, using natural and sympathetic methods whenever possible, and avoiding any violent tools when we can, we might also arrive at our destination with all our layers intact. Our journey too might be slow, frustrating and sometimes upsetting, but it is a journey undertaken in complete co-operation with our own inbuilt guidance system. Ideally our journey becomes one that could eventually help restore the health and happiness that are the birthrights of each one of us.

Checklist

1 Are you ready to consider that some form of 'invisible energy' exists that is the basis for all matter??? Read up on a bit of Einstein or Deepak Chopra (Quantum Healing) to challenge your limiting beliefs.

2 Is it possible that you are ignoring the cause of your illness, dealing mainly with the symptoms of it instead?

3 Prevention is one of the best forms of cure. Look for

opportunities to reduce the levels of stress in your life – WHEREVER POSSIBLE. This could be where you are inflicting damage on yourself that could have long-term repercussions.

4   Are you trusting the voice of your emotions/intuition/instincts enough? Are you really listening? Try making decisions today based on a better balance between feeling and intellect.

5   What might your illness be telling you about your self? Look for the meaning within it.

6   Cancer is a word – not a sentence.

7   Think about the Russian doll – wherever possible try to use gentle tools and a ton of patience for healing.

3

The Perfect Start

*"...And the treasure of your infinite depths would be
revealed to your eyes...
For self is a sea boundless and measureless."*

Kahlil Gibran,
The Prophet

By now you've maybe accepted the idea that you
might benefit from taking more responsibility for your
own health and happiness. Perhaps you've also taken
on board the concept that the answers to some of your
problems could lie inside yourself and not outside.
This is all very well but if it's true then how do you
access these answers? Where do you start in your
attempt to locate this so-called inner guidance?

This is where we're going to have to talk about the

controversial 'M' word. No – it's nothing to do with James Bond's boss. The 'M' word refers to meditation.

So just why is it controversial? Why do some people glaze over the second you mention it, or raise their eyebrows in that "I've-got-a-feeling-you're-going-to-try-to-get-me-to-join-some-dodgy-sect" sort of way?

The first reason is clearly because of the religious or mystical connotations that most people associate with the word (a typical reaction to our suggestion that a client learns how to meditate is usually something like "Aaaaaaargh"). Well we're not part of any particular sect or religion and we're not trying to get you to join us so let's put that one to bed.

The second reason that it is controversial however is because of the scientific debate that rages about the techniques of meditation and the positive effects that they either do or do not produce in and on the human body. Let's look a little closer at all this.

Research On Meditation

Perhaps it's sensible to start from the scientific point of view and see if we can de-mystify meditation a little. After all we'd all be much happier to practise something that wasn't in any way scary. The Transcendental Meditation (TM) organisation (to which the authors have no affiliation) has carried out a considerable amount of sound scientific research into the effects of practising its own version of mantra technique (silent repetition of a word whilst sitting still with eyes closed). A five-year study in the USA in the 1970's examined the health and medical records of two thousand regular TM meditators compared with well-matched control groups. The TM group needed considerably less surgical and medical treatment in all seventeen diseases studied. There were 87% fewer hospital admissions for heart disease, 87% fewer for nervous disorders and 55% less for tumours.

Results of research into TM have been so impressive that not only doctors but also insurance companies have had to re-evaluate their views of meditation. In Britain this evidence prompted a successful campaign by seven hundred doctors to have TM made available on the NHS, although few people seemed aware of this. Perhaps even more surprisingly BUPA reduced their premiums by 15% to TM participants (NB: this discount was available only to TM participants because it was only the TM movement that had been able to organise the research studies that have contributed such evidence). A health insurance company in Holland went even further by reducing their premiums by 40%. Pretty impressive considering insurance companies aren't known to be the greatest risk-takers in the world.

Because of growing awareness of this research, throughout the world many businesses have introduced the practice of meditation into their daily routines as they find their employees become more efficient, less stressed and better decision-makers.

Understanding Brainwaves

But why does meditation have such dramatic effects on people's health, well-being and efficiency? We're now going to talk about brain waves, but don't worry – it will be in terms simple enough for anyone to understand.

It is commonly accepted that there are four basic brainwave types, called Alpha, Beta, Delta and Theta. The ones we produce most of the time are Beta (action mode) and Delta (deep sleep). Most of us are not producing very much Alpha (relaxed but effortlessly alert), or Theta (dreaming, or meditative and deeply calm). This is where meditation comes in.

If you're leading a busy, stressful life (i.e. a 'normal' life in our culture) and not meditating regularly, chances are you're in Beta mode most of the time, which is a state of wakeful, high concentration and ready for action. Sound at all familiar? You wake up out of your deep, Delta sleep, leap straight into Beta mode and don't stop until you fall into bed at the end of the day and drop into Delta sleep again with a little added Theta dreaming time thrown in which you generally don't remember.

So what's so important about these other two types? Let's examine them a little more closely. Alpha waves are produced when we are awake and alert but also relaxed and not experiencing stress. This state is necessary for immune system repair and creative problem solving. Experienced meditators who have been wired up to EEG machines to measure their brainwaves are found to be producing more Alpha and Theta waves than non-meditators in the normal waking state.

During meditation the breathing slows, often to a point that would not have been thought possible prior to meditating. Metabolic activity is also greatly reduced – this being the process during which the body eats up oxygen. The difference between this and sleep, where oxygen consumption is also reduced, is that during sleep the decline is slower and the reduction in consumption of oxygen is less. In other words you reach a more profound state of rest during meditation than you do during a night's sleep. Maybe this is why so many insomniacs who try meditation experience significant improvements in their sleep patterns.

The new condition that this creates is not only very restful, but it also conserves bodily energies and allows a natural breathing space for repairs and recovery to take place. In addition to this, during meditation the levels of chemicals in the blood such as cortisol and lactate are reduced – chemicals that are commonly associated with states of anxiety and stress. Theta waves, produced during deep meditative states, are thought to access the subconscious – the layer between the conscious and unconscious mind. Healing can take place more easily during this theta state as the mind and body are rested and refreshed. Suppressed emotions and memories are released effortlessly and naturally.

All of which we're sure gives you a good list of reasons to get yourself motivated to practice meditation regularly.

"What lies behind us and what lies before us are tiny matters compared to what lies within us."

Ralph Waldo Emerson

Not quite there yet? Okay, there's more – and this bit is pretty mind-blowing. If you're still at all nervous about the thought of meditating because of its mystical connotations, how about replacing the word meditation with the word 'resting'? Could you handle a bit of extra rest every day? Why? Read on.

Rest Versus Meditation

Recent research has compared the physiological effects of meditation in experienced meditators to that of non-meditators simply resting without distractions. Interestingly, the physical effects appear to be extremely similar (cue howls of outrage from experienced meditators practising specific techniques). We were a bit put out ourselves when we first came across this research. However, we now think this is quite exciting news. Why? It's relevant here to tell you our own story of how we have become practitioners and teachers of meditation.

OUR STORY

Ten years ago we decided to learn meditation (we chose TM since their results were so impressive) due to a build up of stressful factors in our lives (two small children, being self-employed, parental ill-health etc etc). We began to practise regularly and soon noticed improvements in our mental and physical states.

The first thing we became aware of was how chronically exhausted we were. For example, Winnie nearly always fell asleep when she tried to meditate (we now know how common this is!); as she persisted with meditation she also found herself sleeping many more hours per week than normal. This would have been a problem if it had lasted, but after about three months she suddenly experienced a dramatic increase of energy and her need for sleep returned to normal.

We also noticed changes for the better in our breathing; our concentration improved and our ability to tolerate alcohol (previously unhealthily high) decreased dramatically even though we were not trying to reduce our intake. Winnie had also been a moderate smoker but lost all desire for cigarettes after a few months. The desire hasn't returned since. Barry became increasingly aware of an underlying health problem and this awareness enabled him to find ways to heal this condition over the following year or so.

The above summarises the immediate and noticeable effects of meditation, but over the years there have been cumulative, positive effects on our general health, energy levels and sense of well-being that have made us as unlikely to miss our twice-daily sessions as we would a meal or brushing our teeth.

More Heresy

But to return to that research about rest periods being just as effective as meditation – surely this is heresy? Perhaps we would have dismissed it, as we're sure many advocates of meditation always will – if it weren't that our own experience bears out this theory. For many years now we have ceased to practise meditation as taught to us by TM – in other words we hardly ever use mantra any more. One could just as well define what we do in our two twenty minute daily 'meditations' as periods of rest in which we organise no distractions, i.e. we don't answer the phone or doorbell and take whatever steps are necessary to ensure that we aren't disturbed.

Various experts and gurus would probably say that we would have achieved increasingly better results if we had persevered with our mantra – but our own inner guidance is that we don't need that specific technique at this time and haven't needed it for many years. It was a great discipline for us as beginners and we'd definitely recommend it, but we now feel just as much benefit at every level – mind, body and spirit – as we ever did when using a technique.

How are we doing with making meditation sound less scary and imposing? Better we hope – after all, now you can just say you're resting and no one will think you've become weird or joined a cult (as Winnie's mum did). Of course this could equally work against you as nobody in our culture thinks resting is of any value – in fact quite the contrary; our puritan work ethic is militantly against resting which is how we've ended up so stressed out in the first place! But at least you have the choice – whichever works best for you – and the results are likely to be the same. As for whether you try 'proper' meditation techniques – that also is up to you, for there is a vast array of information out there to choose from and you can spend a lifetime exploring it.

Motivation And Discipline

Our conclusion based on personal experience, which ultimately of course is the only thing we can ever really base anything on, is that successfully reaping the rewards of meditation (or whatever) is 99.9% down to motivation and discipline, and 0.1% to technique. It's quite a challenge to make time in our days in which we will not allow ourselves to be distracted from silence and stillness.

Resistance To Peace

We also want to investigate why many people may still be resistant to doing this thing – whether you call it meditation, time out, resting, chilling or just the gentle Art of Not Doing. Why is it so hard to give ourselves this gift if it's as wonderful as it's cracked up to be?

Let's backtrack to what we said earlier about those brainwaves called Theta; the ones most people aren't finding the time to produce due to such frantically busy lives. We mentioned that when you reach a place of deep, reflective calmness there can be a release of suppressed emotions and/or memories, sometimes long-buried. An innocuous enough statement perhaps, but think about it. Think about what most people are really up to with all this busy-ness. Could it be possible that the very thought of being still with their feelings, emotions and memories is too frightening? Could it be that they're worried about having to face uncomfortable truths or painful feelings if they stop what they're doing and spend a little time just being? Does their own busy-ness provide them with a convenient comfort zone in which they can safely ignore the quieter voice of their inner guidance?

We believe there must be some truth in this as we have observed the resistance to practising meditation in so many people who have sought our help for the stress in their lives. In many ways it's easier, or at least in some ways more comfortable, to stay stressed out than it is to find out what's really going on inside yourself. But here's another exciting bit. When you allocate time to yourself during your waking, alert state you are also providing a totally safe space for that old 'stuff' to be released. Whether this old energy gets released as a thought, a flood of tears, a laughing fit or a flash of inspiration is impossible to predict. But what is certain is that by giving yourself the room to process these emotions and experiences, you will feel far more in control of things that previously may have been festering.

Imagine your life is like the contents of a pressure cooker. Up to this point you may have been the type of person who has tried not to get angry, who has not really grieved for loved ones, who has not expressed true emotions or who has coped with life whilst resenting many people and your run of bad luck etc etc. All the time these negative feelings are not acknowledged in some way it is like putting a lid on the pressure cooker and locking the valve so nothing can escape.

It is of course inevitable that over time the pressure will build up, unless you find a way of releasing it. This is where periods of rest or meditation are so important. They become the equivalent of lifting the lid or releasing the valve on your own internal pressure cooker.

HENRY

Henry was suffering from anxiety and panic and had been diagnosed schizophrenic by a doctor and psychiatrist. He was twenty two years old and it appeared he had been sliding downhill over the preceding four years. He was on a very high dose of drugs for his condition, a situation that seemed likely to continue throughout his life.

Henry was introduced to meditation immediately and encouraged to read some of the scientific evidence that indicates the physical benefits of meditating. He was impressed, although because of the drugs he was on he found it very difficult to take in much of this information.

As he continued to meditate, so Henry began to find that his mind was becoming a little clearer as to what he wanted and what things upset him. This clarity he found very encouraging.

Being however a typical young man impatient to run before he could walk, he would lapse often from meditating, picking up his recreational drugs and old bad habits. The truth began to dawn on him however that when he stopped working on himself, when he ceased meditating and stopped thinking about things that would make him feel good, he found he sank very easily back into his old depressed, anxious ways.

This experience told him that he could change things negatively or positively by his own choices. He was excited to discover that as he focused on the things that made him feel good and as he continued to meditate, so he found that the things he didn't want in his life began to subside. His need for constant support lessened as he found new strength and desire to live within himself.

A few weeks later he reported feeling happier more often than feeling depressed.

Within a few months he was taken off his medication entirely by his doctor and psychiatrist who both advised him to keep up with his meditating. He immediately felt the benefits of a clearer, drug-free mind. Should he remain free of treatment the NHS will have been saved many thousands of pounds. In addition the State may no

**longer need to support him for the rest of his life due
to the decline that had previously seemed inevitable.**

Checklist

1 Meditation (or rest) needs to be regular to be effective – two twenty-minute sessions a day ideally.

2 You'll more easily overcome your resistance to practising if you remind yourself that it's just that old comfort zone tempting you to stay busy, busy, busy.

3 There's a lot of information out there on this subject; it's well worth doing your own research on it and trying out different techniques.

4 Ask yourself what you have to lose by trying this (apart from a few minutes a day out of your busy-ness).

5 Finding time without distractions in a busy life means taking your own needs seriously and you probably aren't used to doing that. Be gentle with yourself and don't beat yourself up if your practice

is less than regular to begin with – but do persevere!

6 If you can't allow yourself to do two twenty minute sessions everyday, try to do at least one. Anything is better than nothing. Remember the positive physiological changes start to kick in after only a short time.

4

The Right Kind Of Help

"Disease will never be cured or eradicated by present materialistic methods, for the simple reason that disease in its origin is not material."

Dr Edward Bach,
Heal Thyself

Choosing Holistic Therapies

So far we've talked about the importance of taking responsibility and the potential of the self-healing abilities that we all possess. Now that you've started to open up to this new dimension of health, you might want to start looking at the holistic help that is available to complement your self-healing techniques.

The choice of therapies and self-help books is vast, not to say overwhelming, and this is where the use of your intuition will come in handy. This book aims to give only a basic explanation of how holistic/complementary medicine works. Doing justice to individual therapies, experts or books by in-depth exploration would fill volumes.

Meaning Of Holistic

'Holistic' is a much misused and misunderstood term. So what does 'holistic' really mean and what relevance might holism have for our health? We found these definitions of holistic:

1 Looking at the whole system rather than just concentrating on individual components. The overall sum can be greater than a simple totalling of the individual parts, because the 'system' adds something in addition. Another term is 'systems thinking'.

2 Viewing a system as greater than the sum of its component parts. i.e.: $2 + 2 = 5$.

Our understanding of holistic in relation to health and the individual is that the patient is seen as a whole person – mind, body and emotions as one. A holistic approach also seems to imply that proper functioning of the individual parts enables the system itself to add something extra.

The question then becomes "How can we apply a holistic approach for a beneficial result with our health"?

In a truly holistic approach, all aspects of an organism are understood to be as important as each other. Why? Because it is only when all the individual parts work together in harmony that the full potential of the whole can be realised. Rather like the ingredients that make up a cake. Individually they have limited potentials but blend them together in the right proportions and the possibilities become infinite.

So the idea of holistic health can be summarised: if an individual creates a strong and healthy balance between all the aspects that contribute to his or her life, then the 'whole' is likely to benefit from the added extra something that gets created once these individual parts are in harmony. The emotional well-being of that person is considered to be just as important as any particular physical symptoms. It is therefore quite different from the approach of modern medicine, which often tends to treat the symptoms in isolation.

However the two disciplines of holistic and orthodox medicine don't have to be regarded as mutually exclusive. The term 'complementary' often used instead of or in conjunction with holistic, also means that the holistic therapy can benefit the patient alongside their conventional medical treatment.

TERRY

Terry had been diagnosed with acute depression following the sale of his business. Sleep was badly disrupted, his physical health started to suffer, he lost his appetite and suffered from the onset of panic attacks. Emotionally, he became very highly strung.

Anti-depressants were prescribed and Terry started to take them. Besides this medication he was offered little other support and would have to wait weeks for an appointment with a local NHS counsellor. He and his wife started to investigate holistic therapies and he started having some life-coaching and acupuncture as well as improving his nutritional intake by taking up juicing. He had already meditated for many years but was currently finding meditation a real challenge as he was scared to spend time alone.

Whilst the acupuncture got to work on helping him to re-balance at an energy level, the life-coaching helped him to embrace the massive change he had just gone through with his work. We encouraged him to embrace his fears in the present moment rather than trying to 'fix' everything. He began to practise very brief meditations in the presence of his wife as a way of 'dipping his toes in the water of solitude'.

Learning to take very small steps, which just started with accepting the fact that he had just sold his business and didn't as yet have any answers as to his future path, he began to feel a little more at peace. We gave him the affirmation "I accept that I have a problem with not knowing what my future holds" to repeat every day. Rather than trying to find the perfect solution for the future, he began to ground himself in the truth of the present. The acupuncture and juicing continued and he gently increased the time he spent alone with his own thoughts.

As his acceptance of the present grew, so his panic ("I must stop feeling bad right now") subsided. With the help of his doctor he was able to reduce his anti-depressants and this helped him to

become even clearer as to what were the next steps to take. He used holistic treatments to help him to become clearer and effect a greater internal balance that ultimately has lead to a life free of pills and depression. An exciting work opportunity came up and three years later he is still in that job.

A quick word on Terry's meditation experience is worth adding here. Terry had been meditating for years and this had doubtless helped him throughout life with both improved physical well-being and mental clarity. However when this identity crisis arose following the sale of his business, his pain was not meant to be avoided simply by doing a bit of meditation. Terry had to learn to embrace all aspects of himself; he had to find out who he was without his business identity. The reason he was struggling with the meditation was that he was scared that in those moments of silence he might discover that there was nothing there. That he may find someone with no identity, no opinions, and no life.

Ultimately this is never the truth and that's why learning to embrace pain and fear can be so rewarding – because your truth always becomes clear.

Internal Medicines

You could say that holistic therapies are disciplines that work with Nature rather than beating her into submission. As in meditation, they assist the body in releasing its own powerful medicines. They are not, however, a replacement for meditation as they can provide us with neither the deep rest nor the levels of stored energy that cumulative meditation is able to create.

What do we mean by internal medicines? Here's our take on the inner medicine cabinet. Take for example a headache that disappears before you've grabbed the aspirin. It is your internal painkillers that alleviate the pain. The headache doesn't just go of its own accord. The pain was caused in the first place by an imbalance at an energy level and the body responds to the imbalance and attempts to correct it. This is an instance of the body's inbuilt intelligence at work.

Sometimes the message of an imbalance may be blocked from reaching our internal first-aid kit. In these instances, a good holistic practitioner can help significantly in making sure that the way is made clear for the message to be received and for the body to carry out its own repairs.

The Culture Of The Quick Fix

However, just as it is perfectly possible that some symptoms will disappear overnight, so it is also possible that others will barely seem to improve with holistic help. At this point, if you're not already using orthodox medicine as well, it is tempting to run to the nearest GP and ask to be fixed. Patience is needed – big time. Frustration at what appears to be a lack of results can often lead us into major doubts and fears ("what if this is really serious", "what if I'm dying?" etc) about the direction in which our health is going.

We live in a world where, after all, we have come to expect instant results. Holistic medicine cannot always provide this, not necessarily because of any failing on its behalf but more likely because our bodies' inbuilt intelligence knows that an instant result would not be in our best interests. We're suggesting that it is possible that people become ill for a reason. This idea is accepted by many nowadays as the simple truth. Others still regard it as an alien concept.

If it's the truth, then meditation and natural therapy may help us uncover this reason if we give them the chance. If we 'dynamite' the illness out of our system with heavy treatment before looking for a deeper significance, it is not only likely that we will cause further damage elsewhere, but more importantly we may fail to learn the lesson.

Let's go back to the Russian doll. The only way to reach the doll in the middle is to take off each layer one after the other. When we allow healing to build from within, our internal guidance system is taking control and it is possible that it knows in exactly what order problems need to be corrected.

This might well mean that a highly trained holistic practitioner will prescribe some treatments that will appear to do nothing. We're not denying that there are charlatans and quacks out there but your lack of instant results may not be because the treatment itself is ineffective, but because your inner guidance is rejecting it on the basis that there is a better course to follow. It may well be that the treatment itself was not even wrong, just that the timing of the treatment was wrong.

Losing our attachment to an instant cure is a major part of fully accepting holistic treatment (as well as using your intuition and common sense to find reputable practitioners). This attachment is particularly difficult to lose when we are suffering in some way and the distressing symptoms fail to disappear overnight (see Chapter 8 – Coping With Setbacks). But try to remember that it is possible that we have every illness for a purpose and that it could be bringing an opportunity for deeper self-knowledge.

WINNIE TELLS HER STORY

I was suffering from chronic exhaustion and poor immune resistance after the extremely traumatic birth by emergency caesarean of our second daughter (the birth of our first daughter only two years previously had been almost as traumatic). I'd only ever used orthodox medicine and was both ignorant and sceptical about 'alternative' therapies. However, I knew that there was not much more my GP could do to help me and I felt on the brink of serious depression about my poor health and lack of energy to cope with the demands of life with a baby and toddler.

So in desperation I went to the library and came home with a pile of books about all the holistic therapies I could find. Before I could find out very much about any of them, I got acute mastitis. I did not want antibiotics as these would have been passed into the baby. A friend recommended a homoeopath, and I was able to get an appointment with her very quickly. On meeting this therapist I was struck by her confidence and palpable absence of fear. In that moment I realized for the first time how fearful the doctors I had come into contact with throughout my life had been; it seemed to me that doctors trusted neither the human body's healing abilities nor their own treatments very much.

The homeopath quietly assured me that the remedy she would give me would "knock the problem on the head very quickly". The mastitis duly vanished within 24 hours. I was astonished and so impressed that I went back to the same practitioner, whose treatments over the next few months helped me to start to improve my general health. This also inspired me to study holistic therapies in general, to learn meditation and begin a journey of exploration in healing that continues to this day.

Learning Process

Whilst holistic medicine can help us to heal, it can't prevent the process through which we are meant to learn. That process is more likely controlled by our inner intelligence that may be trying to guide us through the necessary steps of unravelling dis-ease. If we try to bypass that process by curing or suppressing the symptom only, it seems likely that we will have to face more dis-ease in the future until we understand the real cause.

One of the problems you face when you choose to adopt the holistic approach is peer pressure. Comments from family and friends such as – "You don't want to trust that witch doctor stuff", or "Shouldn't you be back at work by now?" or "Well you don't look any better", or "What do you mean, you need to have a sleep?"– may do nothing to boost your confidence that you're doing the right thing.

However, if you really learn to listen to yourself, you will get the guidance that you seek. You will know if your attitude to illness is starting to improve, even though there may still be some distressing symptoms. You will know whether you are starting to move in the right direction. It is that knowing which holds the key to your future health. Because once you believe that you are starting to heal yourself, that belief increases, your strength increases and the dis-ease that once ruled your life starts to lose its grip.

The mind is a tool that is not to be underestimated. It is through it that we are able to create what we want and so it is important that we each stimulate it in a way that pleases us as individuals. We all respond differently to different things and it is the power of our emotional responses that may hold the key to healing. The best form of treatment for one person will therefore not necessarily be the best form of treatment for someone else.

So where to start in finding your ideal therapy? You could check out your local library and/or find a bookshop with a good self-help section. Everyone is drawn to specific types of help and you can let yourself be guided in this way. If you feel very strongly about any particular therapy, then it's worth finding out information about local practitioners even to the point of discussing your particular problem with one or two to see what they would recommend and how their treatment would differ.

The following story further illustrates how vibrational medicine (being therapies such as homoeopathy and flower essences that operate at the non-physical or energy levels) can work through different layers of problems to help you unravel dis-ease.

PAMELA

Pam had an area of thickening in her breast that had been present long enough (nearly three months) for her doctor to order more detailed investigations. The previous year her mother had died of breast cancer, so she was understandably very frightened.

Pamela was a mother of three young children and was permanently tired. Her own health, the loss of her mother, plus a recent serious illness suffered by her father, had combined to leave her feeling desperately low and "stressed out" to use her own words.

She was introduced to meditation and vibrational medicine (in this case homeopathy and flower essences).

A detailed picture was built up of her emotional and physical state. The practitioner chose to focus first on her chronic conditions of stress, tiredness and neuralgia as these negative states were preventing Pamela from being able to find any form of balance.

The combination of meditation, coaching and remedies started to energise Pamela. After only a few weeks she reported that a long-standing back pain had reduced considerably. Sleep patterns improved. Anxiety reduced. As a result she was feeling much more optimistic.

Pamela began to experience a feeling of being in control of her health for the first time since she could remember. The improvements continued and in time the thickening in her breast also disappeared. She returned to the hospital for a mammogram (breast X-ray). The tests gave her health the all-clear and Pamela's request for a medical interpretation of what had happened resulted in a bemused Consultant commenting that "I can only attribute it to female hormones".

Checklist

1 Accepting that healing comes from within doesn't mean you have to do it all by yourself and can't get help. There's a lot of wonderful help out there.

2 You might need to do some research but remember

to use your intuition to be guided to the right therapy.

3 Learn to stay with your pain/fear. Be aware of the attachment to a 'Quick Fix' – remember patience is usually necessary when you allow healing to happen in a natural way.

4 Dis-ease is in your life for a reason – it brings an opportunity to learn.

5

Resistance To Change

*"Each old layer must give way in order to be replaced
with new thinking. Some of it is easy, and some of it is like
trying to lift a boulder with a feather."*

Louise L Hay,
You Can Heal Your Life

The Oxford dictionary defines 'resist' as follows:
"Resist. v & n. v.t. stop course of, withstand action or
effect of, prevent from reaching or penetrating..."

Habits And Their Origins

Let's face it; we're all creatures of habit. Our habits,
our daily routines, our thoughts and beliefs crystallize
over a period of time and depend very much upon the
influence of people who are close to us. These beliefs

about ourselves can go back for generations and very likely haven't much to do with our feelings in the here and now.

Some of this inherited thinking may be in our best interests, For instance some good things to have passed down to us might be healthy eating habits, life skills or positive moral values. However some of this 'conditioning' can be very limiting and, in some cases, undoubtedly damaging. Examples of negative conditioning might include a tendency to depend on drugs/alcohol or an inability to communicate feelings or manage relationships.

It is very common to find that, as you start to make progress, you begin to identify your real problems which in turn bring out a strong resistance from within. This resistance is your unwillingness to instigate change in the ideas and lifestyle habits to which you've become accustomed.

This resistance to change is one of the biggest barriers to healing. That's why it's important to recognise where the resistance is coming from and how relevant it is to your particular position right now. Whether you've consciously or unconsciously placed this barrier here or whether it's the result of a generations-old belief, the goal has to be to transcend it and move on. Giving up and turning back will result in the end of your progress and will possibly put an end to your ability to heal yourself fully. The only realistic way forward is to overcome it.

CARRIE

Carrie was in her sixties and suffering from rheumatoid arthritis. She had begun a course of holistic treatment including counselling. During this counselling treatment it became clear that she felt completely restricted at home as a result of the way in which her new husband's children had reacted to her becoming their new 'mother' (the 'children' were in their thirties and forties). When her husband was not in the same room, they were abusive and rude. As a result she felt unable to move, scared to go out even. She felt paralysed with fear. Her body seemed to be reflecting this mental torture.

There seemed little doubt that Carrie needed to broach this subject with her husband. Unfortunately she felt unable to discuss this with him, scared of how he might react. She gave up the counselling and returned to her life of pain. The

resistance to change was too overwhelming for her to overcome.

As you become more honest with yourself and more aware of what makes you happy or unhappy, you might also begin to notice that there are things about your life that suddenly don't seem right. This simple recognition comes through your emotions, your feelings – and worryingly your guidance seems to be directing you towards conflict. How can conflict be a part of healing? Understandably, the fearful part of yourself might want to retreat from this conflict just like Carrie did in the last story. Why on earth should you face confrontation when you can avoid it by retreating?

Change – The Ouch Factor

The conflict that causes such a fearful response is change. As we've said already, we're all creatures of habit and change is something that we are almost designed to "resist". We're making progress and yet one part of us wants to "stop the course of" that progress, because all of a sudden it involves making changes and change is not something that we like to do as it's potentially painful.

Making the right changes however is what healing is all about. Remember that it's possible that nobody gets any illness without a reason. However difficult this may still be for you to accept, it must be considered at least a possibility if you want to remain open to a change in your dis-ease. Accepting this possibility gives you the power to look for the reason. Once identified, you can learn from it and make whatever changes are necessary. As you follow the steps described so far you may be getting closer all the time to that reason or reasons and as you get closer so you'll be made aware of things that you need to change if you are to progress. Conquering our resistance to change may well be a key factor in complete healing.

Some people want to give up on self-healing as soon as they meet any resistance. The reason is that they are scared of changing what may be a small or large aspect of their life. Take employment as an example. People are often dissatisfied, consciously or unconsciously with their job and working environment. Very often they are under great pressure every day and yet they seem to receive little job satisfaction other than the financial returns. Ask them why they do it and they will invariably say because they need the money.

Another more complex category contains those people who are in a job for which they believe they are well suited. These jobs might be highly exciting, highly paid and highly stressful. It's not unusual for someone to be unable to see that their moments of personal glory come nowhere near to making up for the many moments of negative pressure and high stress.

CHARLIE

Charlie was head of sales for a leading city company. A married man in his early forties he had recently had a major health scare and had missed much time at work due to ill-health. A high achiever, he continually drove himself to unreasonable lengths to meet ever-increasing targets. His health and family suffered from this and his work was beginning to suffer too but his addiction to 'the kill' had pushed him to the point at which his body had just said 'no more' (... to be continued)

Whether you fall into either of the categories mentioned or whether your dis-ease stems from something else, when you start asking for help your internal wisdom will give you plenty of clues as to where to look. Your recognition of the cause of disease is only hampered when you choose to shut your eyes to certain possibilities. As the cumulative effects of meditation start to take effect and as you gather new information from other sources, so you'll begin to realise that you have only to keep an open mind to all possibilities to make the changes that may bring about self-healing.

A Slight Shift In Attitude

For instance in the employment examples listed earlier you may find that you do not need to change jobs so much as to change your approach to the job. You may be resenting your work every day because you have to do it to pay the mortgage. If you question yourself fully, if you answer yourself honestly, you'll know whether this job is what you really want to be doing. If it is, then you need to change your attitude by going to work every day reminding yourself that this is what you really want to do, not just what you have to do.

If however you know deep down that the job itself is wrong for you, delaying facing that decision can only serve to cause you more dis-ease. It is the same with a relationship and it is the same with any activity in life. If you're doing something regularly that is not in harmony with what you really want to be doing, then you must stop doing it if you want to avoid further dis-ease.

'Positive Stress?'

It is worth noting at this point that our definition of stress always means that which is unwanted – we often hear people referring to positive stress or saying that they need stress. It is possible that they mean they want challenges or enjoy working to tight deadlines or enjoy the excitement of dangerous activity. However, when any activity reaches a point beyond challenge and becomes more than the individual can cope with, then that activity becomes stressful. That cut-off point might be different for each one of us, but when it is being reached regularly then we surely must change the activity or risk paying the price of dis-ease.

Small Steps

As we have said, you will be given many clues as to what parts of your life, if any, need to change. Quite often you'll know, without having to receive any further guidance. For those for whom it is that clear, it is then a question of deciding what to do about these troubled areas. From within this book we cannot advise on whether it is just a question of changing an attitude to someone or something, or of leaving a whole situation behind. What we can say is that, unless one hundred percent certain, it is worth making small changes to begin with to see what that leads you to. If you're going the right way, you'll find that more doors open in front of you and that, in spite of that scary old 'ouch' factor when making the first changes, life becomes easier and more joyful.

CHARLIE (continued)

At the beginning of Charlie's first session with us he was asked "If there is one thing you could change in your life right now, what would it be?"

It took a few minutes and several questions from him before he understood that we were talking about any problem – not just one that related to

work. After the feelings of guilt subsided (taking work time to discuss a personal issue) – he opened up about some domestic concerns and health worries that were causing him stress.

It was suggested to him that if he took very small steps and learnt how to deal positively with these personal issues, if he felt good about his contribution as a father and partner then he would start to benefit from a far better state of mind. It's a simple rule: come into work feeling good about yourself and you'll perform better. It's not rocket-science. It's logic. It works.

Within a couple of weeks he had already started to make changes. He began coming into work at 9.00am instead of 8.00am and he was now leaving for home at 5.30-6.00pm instead of working in a daze until 9.00pm.

As the weeks went on positive changes increased, changes that he felt able to sustain (unlike many techniques he had received on sales courses which seemed to fade after just a few days).

He started driving into work, which cost him a little more money but gave him a more relaxed beginning and end to each day; for the first time ever he didn't take his laptop away on holiday. Instead of chasing after every deal, he started to recognize which ones to let go of and which to pursue.

Within three months of his first meeting with us, he closed the biggest of any UK deal done by his company during the previous 6 month period and at the same time his pipe-line (potential future deals) improved dramatically. His physical well-being improved beyond all recognition as did his confidence in his ability to remain healthier. His home life reached a level of happiness that he and his wife had not thought possible in the stressful world of City finance. And his children now have a father who is able to find time to play with them almost every night.

Going Deeper

For those however who are not certain about the true causes of dis-ease, who have ideas but are afraid that they may be wrong, a more detailed assessment of their position in life in the present moment is necessary.

It's a big step to admit to yourself that everything in life is not perfect and that something needs to change. But, without that conviction, without the very firm belief that there is anything in life that needs changing, there's not much point in spending any time trying to improve. After all, if everything is perfect why bother changing?

Willingness To Change

The above question needs to be considered, meditated upon and absorbed. The significance of accepting the need to change is far weightier than it may appear. It's even more significant when you take into account that this willingness to change seems to be most powerful if it is unconditional. If you can accept that anything and everything in your life may need to change in some way, shape or form, our experience tells us that you are more likely to achieve positive results.

Accepting this notion, that nothing in your life at present is certain of remaining exactly the same, takes time to adjust to. We all tend to fear for what we have already got when anybody mentions change. We fear the unknown. We fear loss. In consultations the authors often find when talking about accepting change that people react by imposing conditions, saying something like "...well, I'm prepared to contemplate change in this area of my life, but not in that one".

Unconditional Surrender

But the very nature of life on earth suggests that we all need to accept the possibility of change in anything. Deepak Chopra calls this "living in the wisdom of uncertainty"[1]. Our experience tells us that nothing, nothing that is in our highest interests to have, will be taken away from us. Things that at present you cannot foresee being any better than they are can become immeasurably improved when you give them the opportunity of change. In short, the desirable things in your life can become much better and the unwanted things can disappear. It may not happen overnight, but if you accept the need to change, at least it can happen.

The Car Metaphor

When you're ready to accept the possibility of change in your life, it's a bit like accepting that your car has been going in the wrong direction and you need to hit the brakes. Once you've started to brake, (i.e. started to look for areas in your life that need change) you can relax in the knowledge that the car will eventually

1   "Seven Spiritual Laws of Success" by Deepak Chopra. Published in UK by Excel Books.

stop. But of course the car does not stop immediately – there's a momentum involved which means it has to slow down gradually.

What we're trying to say here is don't expect massive results straightaway – it takes a little while before you come to a complete halt. When you do stop however, your previous journey (i.e. your old approach to life) has now been halted and you can head off in a new direction. You might need to change direction on your new journey many times. Don't ever judge this as being wrong. Each journey is a vital step in bringing you nearer each time to your truth – all the time you're getting more in harmony with your true wants and desires.

Trusting Our Wants

People often say to us that they would feel bad pursuing their own wants and desires. And we reply, well tell us, what is so bad about your own wants? And when people stop and think, they find out that in fact what they want is nothing dreadful, nothing dangerous, nothing anti-social. Quite often they find out that they don't even know what they really want. And it is this sorry fact that brings unhappiness to them and those around them. Our dreams, our wants and desires are the very keys that start our car. What good is a car with no keys?

So, how do you find those keys, or how do you hit those brakes on a car that is going in the wrong direction?

You can be guided, but nobody else can do it for you. You can be shown where the pedal is, but only you can hit it. It's all a question of choice. The key lies in your willingness to accept change unconditionally. A method for recognising your fears and wants is to carry out the following simple exercise:

'Transforming Fear Into Positive Creating'

If you have been experiencing dis-ease of any kind, you have probably been creating it unconsciously out of fear. People tend at first to deny that they have a lot of fears – sometimes they even deny that they have any fear at all. So your very first step is to admit to yourself that you do have fears.

Once you've summoned the courage to do this – and it does take courage – the next step is to begin writing them down in a list. It is very important to take your time over this because it will help you make a blueprint from which you may ultimately start shaping your perfect life. Start with the most obvious fears and then gradually begin to add to that list. As you write, be aware of the feelings that come up. Very often, this process alone may allow you to see that your fears are not nearly as frightening as you first imagined them to be.

But there's more to it than just looking at the list of fears. The next stage is to take your first fear and turn it into something that you want. Examples:

Fear	Want
I fear the shape/size of my body	*I want to be happy with my appearance/body*
I fear not having enough money	*I want enough money to... (list each thing that you want the money for)*
I fear suffering with my illness	*I want to be at peace with my suffering*
I fear being alone	*I want to be in a happy, long-term relationship*
I fear death/dying	*I want to be at peace with death/dying*

When you feel the list is as complete as possible (you can of course add more at any time in the future as things come up) and after you have turned the fears into wants, you can throw away your list of fears. The objective of this exercise is to recognise the fears, turn them into positive wants and then focus on the wants in as detailed and emotional a way as possible.

Once you start thinking about the things that you really want and if you focus on **feeling the excitement** of what it would be like to have them right now, you are engaging in a powerful form of reality creating. The more detail you give yourself and the Universe, the more chance you have of attracting that very thing to you. However, please pay close attention to the following:

Two Vital Facts

1 You have NO control over anybody else's reality. It is therefore no good trying to create something for somebody else. Examples of this could be:

I want my mother to stop worrying about me
I want my sister to have more money
I want my child/parent/lover to be out of pain
I want my partner to be more loving to me

You have no control over any of the above. You only have control over how you are feeling about the above. The correct wants would therefore be something like:

> *I want to feel relaxed at how my mother reacts to me*
>
> *I want to be at peace with my sister's financial limitations*
>
> *I want to have compassion for my child's/parent's/lover's suffering*
>
> *I want to be happy about my relationship with my partner*

In none of the above do you have any control over the actual reality that each of those other people is experiencing – but you do have complete control over how you feel about their relative conditions/ behaviours. Your power lies in identifying that control – knowing where your responsibilities begin and end – and then using all your energy towards a positive and acceptable result.

This does not mean you suddenly become hard and callous, with not a care for anybody. It does mean you become so focused that you know exactly what you can and cannot do physically and emotionally for others; that you know the boundaries between someone else's pain and your appreciation of it, and that you do not get yourself into stressful conditions about something over which you have no control.

2 You cannot create negatively. This may seem obvious, but it amazes us how many people start their wants lists with "I don't want". This goes against all the laws of the Universe. Examples of this may be:

I don't want to have cancer any more
I don't want to get any fatter
I don't want to suffer in pain any more
I don't want to be lonely any more
I don't want to experience poverty any more

All of these involve creating negatively. Impossible. Can't be done. The correct wants would therefore be something like:

I want to have perfect health
I want to be happy with my body
I want to be able to cope with my suffering
I want to attract fulfilling relationships

*I want to attract enough money to …. (always
specify what you want money for)*

This is positive creating, not negative. Each of the above is therefore possible to make happen (however unlikely it may seem at the moment), because we are all powerful creators. It is only when you try to create negatively that you find your wants remain out of reach. So, please remember, no negative creating.

Once you have created your wants list, continue to add to it, change it, detail it more, until you have a list that gives you a feeling of joy and anticipation.

With this list completed, life will start to have greater clarity. However, as it stands you have a list of desires that exist in some future point. The next step is to learn how to come into the present moment with this information so that your desires can manifest.

The most powerful state of mind in which to manifest your desires is that of self-acceptance. If you are not in a state of conscious acceptance of everything in your reality as it now is, then you will struggle to attract the changes you desire. But how do we create this acceptance? Affirmations are powerful tools to use, but are not much good if you do not **feel** that what you are saying is true.

For instance your want may be to feel good about your bodily appearance. But in the moment you may feel terrible about it – so using an affirmation such as "I have the perfect body" will probably produce feelings of anger or hopelessness within you. You need to make a much smaller step towards acceptance by stating something like "I accept that I have a problem with my appearance". This brings you into the world of acceptance and will help you to start feeling more whole as you accept all the aspects that make you, you.

PLEASE NOTE: this may seem like a trivial or unimportant step but it can be crucial to help you to start the process of positive creation. Why? Because you can waste enormous amounts of time and energy trying to take too big a step because of your attachment to getting quick results. We have seen this happen time and again. We all have a tendency to want a quick fix and we try to make a big jump to get results fast.

Let's go back to the example of wanting to change your body shape. Say you are suffering with self-loathing about your overweight body and therefore you try to use the affirmation "I have the perfect body". You'll find it very hard to believe that this affirmation is doing any good if you can't **feel** any truth in this statement. And if you can't believe it, you're less likely to see it. Believing is seeing. You have to make your affirmation something you can feel as the truth right now. It may seem like a frustratingly small step but you **cannot skip or avoid this stage** and we cannot over-emphasise this enough.

Therefore the next stage of the exercise looks like this:

Want (future)	Affirmation (now)
I want to be happy with my appearance/body	*I accept that I have a problem with my appearance/body*
I want enough money to... (list each thing that you want the money for)	*My needs are being met in the moment* *Or (if you feel that they are not)* *I accept that I have a problem with the state of my finances*
I want to be in control of my suffering	*I accept the pain I am in* *Or (if the pain is too great)* *I accept that I find my pain overwhelming*

Using affirmations in this way will help you to drop any internal fight and to make your first steps into the positive world of acceptance. It is only at this stage of resting in the stillness of acceptance that you will even realise that you have been engaging in a big, exhausting fight with yourself – the fight of non-acceptance of how things are, right now. It is only from this point that you can start to recognise that your fear is no longer so powerful. You will also find it much easier to identify what small steps you can take in the realm of 'doing' to continue to improve your state of being.

Work with this list and your affirmations regularly – refer to it as often as possible so that it becomes a very focused part of your daily awareness. Regular practice is very important. You will soon begin to realise how previously you went through life living in fear.

Opportunities will come along and you will know to take them. Things will start to happen that will make you realise that you are now beginning to work in harmony with the Universe and that as a result the Universe is bringing its magic to you. Just detail those fears, turn them into wants, create your affirmations and enjoy what you start attracting. You are learning to become a conscious creator and there is nothing more magical than the realisation that you **can** create the life you want.

HARRY

Harry was an alcoholic who had attempted suicide on two occasions. He could think of no reason to live at all. He was encouraged to write down all his fears and, although he found this quite difficult to start with, he soon had a list of fifteen fears. These fears included drinking himself into oblivion and losing the respect of his family.

Harry was then shown how to turn these fears into things that he would like to have happen. "I fear losing the respect of my family" turned into "I want to earn my family's respect"; "fear of drinking into oblivion" became "I want to be in control of my desire for alcohol".

Before long, someone who a few minutes previously had no reason to live, now found himself with fifteen powerful reasons for living. And yet nothing in his physical life had changed. It was just a change of perspective. Life became the half full glass as opposed to the half empty glass. Within a few days he had turned his "I want to earn my family's respect" into "I am earning my family's respect" and he supported this by taking action. He went and helped out his oldest brother who was in bed with flu. He cut his grass and did some general gardening. This was the start of a process during which he gradually transformed a fearful situation into one that was far more positive.

Checklist

1   Be aware of old habits and programming that don't serve you and that have become a comfort zone that tempts you not to make changes.

2   Always look to take small steps when attempting change – you will find they lead to more sustainable results and ultimately bigger changes.

3   "Am I really willing to change?" is a most important question to ask yourself and to keep asking yourself. Answer honestly at every stage along your healing journey.

4 If the answer is "yes" then you need to be willing to change unconditionally – you can't fulfil your potential if you're only prepared to accept change in specified areas.

5 If you have started to make changes, have patience and don't expect results straightaway – remember the car metaphor.

6 Learn to identify what you want from life.

6

Universal Laws

"When we understand these laws and apply them in our lives, anything we want can be created..."

Deepak Chopra,
The Seven Spiritual Laws of Success

Universal Laws. What are we on about now, you may well ask? Well, we're not talking about gravity, magnetism or any other laws of physics that you might have been taught at school. And yet what we are talking about may well have just as much significance in your life as any of the above.

A good understanding and sound application of these Universal Laws could help you to transform your life. They will certainly enhance the benefits of self-help techniques. Many of the books that have helped us to change our own lives base their content upon the existence of such laws. Understanding how they work gives a greater understanding of how life itself may work – it is this knowledge that may enable us to create the health and happiness that we seek. Are these truly some of the Laws of the Universe? You decide.

Law 1 – Like Attracts Like (Or Law Of Attraction)

This law is all about your state of being and how you can act as a powerful magnet. It dictates that whatever your current emotional state may be, it is likely to attract more of the same back to you.

We have already explained how much power our emotions may contain. The law of attraction suggests that we will manifest anything that we really put great emotion into –importantly this can include negative things as well as positive things.

Getting into a peaceful, happy state of being therefore becomes of prime importance. Because if we start from a happy place, logic tells us that via the law of attraction we should attract back even more happiness into our lives. So how do we help ourselves to manifest this more balanced state? How do we train ourselves into right-thinking?

Fear Of Lack

What most of us tend to do when we are thinking about something that we really want – such as perfect health, or a fulfilling relationship, or a lovely house – is put our attention on the fear of not getting those things.

Instead of repeatedly saying to ourselves "I want perfect health", or "I want enough money to buy...", we tend to slide into "I'm scared of not getting better", or "what if I don't get enough money". By doing this, our greatest emotion is one of fear; fear of not getting better or not having enough money. This emotion is so strong that it may well attract like towards itself – in this case continuing ill health or poverty.

Once you get into the 'fear of not' state of mind, you may find that you tend to attract even more of those things that you do not want. How many of us for instance have got into debt only to find even more bills and charges appearing as if from nowhere? How many people do you know who seem to be continually drifting from one physical problem to another, or from one relationship crisis to another?

Shift The Emphasis Of Your Thinking

However low or high our morale, very few of us consciously put the right accent on our thought-processes. Just by shifting the emphasis on to what you want and away from what you fear not getting, you could start to reap the rewards as you work in conjunction with this particular Universal Law.

If you can just stop worrying about not getting better or happier, better health or happiness may start to come. As you continue to focus only on having and wanting to have perfect health and happiness, so your health and happiness might start to improve and as long as you continue in this frame of mind you may continue to attract improved health/happiness. Whenever you are knocked back by dis-ease you need only remind yourself of this Universal Law "Like Attracts Like" to know where you must put your thoughts, your emotions.

Remember that regular meditation will help you to achieve a clearer mind, further enabling you to focus attention on the areas that you want to improve.

CARL

Carl had been diagnosed with depression in his late teens. Now in his mid-thirties he had gone through life assuming that he was stuck with this condition and that little could change.

He anticipated a continuation of his depression from year to year as predicted by his doctors and used his anti-depressants as part of a coping strategy rather than believing that he would ever really be cured.

In our first meeting he was asked to change the emphasis of his thinking. To move away from "I fear this condition continuing" and into "I want to feel well enough to...". He was asked what he would like to do if he had total freedom to choose (he was currently in computer data collection). He surprised himself by answering that he'd like to do something involved with walking and people.

We encouraged him to continue focusing on this more positive approach. As he gave himself permission to allow these ideas into his daily thinking, so he found himself in a more confident and happy frame of mind and he began investigating the idea more solidly. Within a few weeks he had researched a career in walking involving education and a couple of months later Carl left the world of computers and became manager of a youth hostel in a beautiful part of the country. His dependence upon his anti-depressants reduced as he found himself able to attract more of those things into his life that he wanted by placing his focus on more positive ideas.

Carl challenged history, turning round the idea that he was doomed to go on with the same old depressed life. He started to think outside the box and allowed in many more positive ideas. He became a different type of magnet. As he felt more inspired so it is possible that he initiated a process that helped him to attract the help he needed to start fulfilling his dreams.

Law 2 – What Goes Around Comes Around

If the first law involves your state of being, then this one is more to do with taking action – the realm of doing.

What you give out, you invariably get back. We can see this from the previous law and we can also see it in a number of other ways that may enable us to focus our attention in the right place.

If you imagine your emotions and your actions are like a boomerang, you can begin to understand how this may work. Every time you give out a strong emotion or take some sort of action that has strong emotion attached to it, you'll find, just like a boomerang, that it will try to come back to you. Some people call this cause and effect.

So how can you use this to aid your physical or emotional recovery and to reach the possible causes of dis-ease? Again, the answer may seem deceptively simple. In your process of removing dis-ease, you need to learn to give out only those things that you would wish to come back to you.

If you want to improve your physical state in time for a certain event (wedding, holiday, important meeting etc), then you need to give yourself the time to heal properly (we cannot stress enough how challenging many people find this to carry out and yet it is a major key in the healing process).

If you want to receive more love from those close to you, then you need to give more love to them.

If you want your children to be more gentle and polite to you and others, then you need to be more gentle and polite to them and to others in front of them.

If you want more money to come to you, then you need to give more money out – even if you only start with small donations or personal treats.

If you want your ideas and beliefs to be more understood and accepted by friends and colleagues, then you need to make extra efforts to understand and accept their ideas and beliefs.

There is however something very important to bear in mind with this. It is not just what we give out that is important. It is also how we give it. Each of the above examples will benefit you even more in the long-term if carried out with strong positive emotion.

Giving Unconditionally

Giving anything – love, money or even information – reaps the greatest rewards when given without conditions. Energy given unconditionally by us often comes back into our lives in the way that will benefit us most at that time. If you say "Okay, I'll pay more attention to my family provided they promise to leave me alone when I need my space" you are making your love conditional upon their behaviour and we're suggesting therefore that you are less likely to get what you want. You're placing the onus on your family to create your life as you want it instead of taking full responsibility yourself. You are in effect giving them power over you – if they fail to deliver the conditions then your life is not as you want it – and you will blame them accordingly.

The reason that it is so important to give these things out without conditions attached is that we have no absolute knowledge now as to how we may need them to be returned in the future. Nature has a way of providing us with what we need at just the time that we most need it. If you've given out gifts, love and help without expecting anything back you'll find that they will return to you in a way and at a time that will be most beneficial.

If however you give out these things with strings attached, either with conditions or even just begrudgingly, you'll find that you may be bound by similar restrictive conditions when they come back. Money that you've given without great joy may fail to bring you great happiness when you later acquire it. Love that has been given conditionally may return to you with more conditions attached.

113

This law states that, quite literally, the more you give the more you get – both in thought and in matter. Remember the important part of this is the emotion that is attached to the giving. If you give things with great joy and love, even if they are only compliments, they will come back to you in abundance and bring you great happiness. Try it – see what comes back into your life.

OUR HOUSE MOVE

After eight years in a beautiful rented house, our landlady informed us that we would have to move out within a short period of time. With social networks firmly established by the whole family in the village in which we lived, we had no desire to move out of the area. And yet rental prices had risen so much and there were so few suitable houses generally available where we wanted to be (our standards were high because of where we had lived for so long and we didn't want to compromise) that a part of us told us this could seem like a hopeless situation if we chose to see it that way.

We knew that the energy we were giving out would be vital in what we could attract back to us.

Although logic told us that a light, quiet house in a beautiful country setting yet within walking distance of the village would not be within our price range (even if it did exist which our intellects also doubted), we held our vision whilst trying not to be too attached to having it. What we specifically did not do was prepare our children for the worst by saying things like "we might have to move out of the village" or "we might have to live in a much darker and smaller house on the main road".

So what did we do? One of the benefits of regular meditation is that a course of action can sometimes become totally clear. A course of action that can sometimes seem illogical. The action that became clear to us at this stage was not to start looking for a new rental property or visiting estate agents, but instead to start 'de-cluttering' our house.

And so it was that we started sorting through years old possessions, giving piles of 'stuff' away to charity shops and friends who would benefit. This was our way of saying to the universe "Okay, we'll prepare ourselves unconditionally to move by making ourselves much lighter, you repay us by providing us with the perfect house."

Within a few weeks we had established a momentum of house clearing. The house felt fantastic. We started cleaning it properly and getting it into good shape to hand back to our landlady who had been so kind to us over the years. We didn't have to work too hard on the fear, although as our intended moving date loomed ever nearer, a little bit of anxiety began to creep in about where we would next live.

This small fear was answered the very next day when Barry's uncle offered to house us for a limited time in his house in the village if nothing else became available. This helped us to relax about a roof over our heads and we continued to empty and clean the house unconditionally.

Within forty-eight hours we found out about a brand new house that would be available exactly when we needed it and which was within easy walking distance to the village. It was in a beautiful setting with views across the valley and had large picture windows giving plenty of light. Being on the fringes of an organic farm it meant that lovely walks were also on the doorstep.

We met with the landlord who seemed to take a shine to us, were offered the house and moved in within four weeks. It seemed to us no less than a miracle – one that we have no doubt was able to happen because we took the action first that would attract back to us the result we wanted. We believed it and then we saw it.

Law 3 – Non-Attachment

It is a fact of life that we all tend to form attachments to certain outcomes in life. On the face of it there seems to be not much difference between wanting to achieve specific goals and having an attachment to reaching those goals. In fact there is a significant difference.

Non-Attachment = Freedom

Let us assume you've got a cold that you'd like to get rid of. If you have found the ideas contained in this book useful, then you'd probably do some extra meditation and rest, possibly get some holistic treatment.

Whether you were attached to the outcome or not, these steps would probably be the same. The big difference comes in the emotion with which you approach the cold. The non-attached person would do all of the above, possibly even using the ideas given in the last chapter, on the basis that he or she is completely accepting and trusting what is going on and has therefore no expectations of the future. All of their energy is going into focusing correctly in the present moment. This non-attachment to an outcome produces no fight, no friction and wastes no energy.

As a result the cold may be allowed to leave the body in its own way, as effortlessly as possible for the individual involved. Whilst he or she obviously wants perfect health to be restored, there is no pressure being placed on a time. The cold is being accepted unconditionally.

Attachment = Fear

The attached person although also wanting to have perfect health, is emotionally imbalanced by the attachment to having to have perfect health by a specific date; let's say a long-awaited holiday or important job interview. This attachment, expressed through their need to get rid of the cold by a certain time, creates in itself a negative emotion that is very powerful; the fear of not getting rid of it by this deadline.

As a result, the fear is the strongest emotion, created out of their attachment to their deadline. Instead of focusing on the present moment, that person is focusing their attention on a future need. They may therefore be wasting their energy worrying about their future health, instead of accepting and trusting their present state of health. The energy loss encourages the cold to linger, disrupting the sufferer's life to a much greater degree than that of the person who fully accepted their cold and focused entirely upon trusting their state of health in the present moment without any attachment to when the cold had to leave.

Non-attachment works with health, relationships, money – in fact any aspect of life. It is one thing to want more money, better relationships or better health; but it is something else altogether to having to have any or all of these things immediately or even within a certain time frame. By telling yourself that you have to have them, you are saying that your life is not acceptable without them. This not only means you're focusing on the future instead of in the present; it also leads you back to the vicious circle, mentioned earlier in the book, of thinking that life is not fair, that you've somehow been unlucky because you don't yet have those things that you think you must have to bring you happiness. Attachment to a future outcome makes us unhappy with our present circumstances and unhappiness seems to be no basis for self-healing.

By accepting exactly where you are right now, by focusing on what you want and by accepting those things that come to you, whether colds or cash, you'll enable the Universal Laws to work for you, which may in turn help to provide you with whatever is in your best interests to have. Because of your acceptance, the right things will come to you with seemingly little effort at times that are best suited to your needs. Losing your attachment to any outcome, good or bad, is another vital step on the path to your goal.

EDWARD

Edward was a professional man in his late fifties and had recently been diagnosed with cancer in two organs. He and his wife had had meetings with two leading consultants and had come away from these meetings feeling pressurised into taking some sort of immediate action; unfortunately the consultants

were both suggesting different courses of action.

Edward had been introduced to the concept of Universal Laws. He was beginning to take the role of the mind in his own healing very seriously. It was suggested to him that he learn first how to focus on what he wanted to achieve in the present moment; at that particular time this was not a 'cure' for that was a longer-term goal. His first objective, and the potential route to healing, was to gain clarity of mind regarding the conflicting advice being recommended by these two consultants.

He learnt to meditate, read more and started being aware of what messages he was giving out to people. To start with he had been desperate (understandably) to do the 'right' thing (i.e. – take the right medical route) – and people were responding to him in an equally desperate way (as shown by the sense of panic and disagreement from the consultants).

Now he was learning the importance of taking the action that 'felt' right at a time that 'felt' right. He focused his attention on choosing the consultant that made him 'feel' good. He attended his next meeting with this consultant in a more focused state of mind.

121

The consultant, possibly responding to Edward's decrease in fear, did not push him into anything. This alone was a significant change from previous meetings. It gave Edward precious time to reflect, read more about his illness and find out more about potential benefits and side effects of the treatment being recommended.

Upon careful consideration of all the information available, Edward and his wife were able to make the choice of treatment that seemed most appropriate to all concerned. A need to satisfy an initial intellectual panic had been replaced by a desire to act in a more careful and considered way.

This story has no magical fairy-tale ending. However, Edward has found that since he has started to understand the significance of Universal Laws he has been able to attract far more of what he wants into his life and far less of what he doesn't want. This he has achieved just by being clear in his own mind as to what he wants out of a given situation. It is inevitable that cancer patients want their cancer to go and Edward is no different. But he is also aware that he cannot possibly judge what he still has to learn from this experience.

Instead of being in a maelstrom of panic he assesses everything clearly and in relation to how he feels. Since becoming aware of the potential of his own thought-processes and the importance of his emotional state, Edward has been able to take life-changing decisions without the effort and anxiety that he would previously have assumed to be inevitable.

Checklist

1   Your state of being acts as a magnet, attracting back to it more of what it is projecting. The more peaceful, positive and happy your general state, the more peace, positive experiences and happiness you will attract to yourself.

2   Action and words also have a cause and effect. Do and speak from a positive, loving place and positive, loving results are more likely to come back to you.

3   Focus positively on whatever you want so that you don't give energy to your fear of lack.

4 Drop your attachment to specific results. Focus your energy on the present moment, don't waste it worrying about the future.

7

Continuing The Improvements

"How can we keep our mind and body in that state of harmony which will make it difficult or impossible for disease to attack us, for it is certain that the personality without conflict is immune from illness."

Edward Bach,
Heal Thyself

Instigating change in aspects of our lives in the present can have dramatic effects upon our health and happiness. You will often start to see the benefits of these effects almost immediately as you begin to understand more fully how your emotions guide you towards certain decisions. Continuing the improvements that those changes bring is the next stage of our journey.

Get To Know Yourself

We've introduced you to the idea that your emotions are the voice of your inner wisdom, or guidance. Because you've probably been brought up to listen mainly to your intellect and not to your feelings and emotions it's vital to take the time to get to know yourself – something which is best achieved through regular meditation as described in Chapter 3. If you find yourself uncertain about important decisions, just asking some relevant questions in your own head and then tuning in to the feeling that comes up as a result of posing possible solutions can often lead you to the guidance you seek.

For example, imagine you're faced with a difficult career decision. If you consider the various possible outcomes, such as staying in your current job, moving to a new job, leaving this type of work altogether and starting up something by yourself – you'll find that one of the options will make you feel better, more excited than the others. It may sound simplistic, but this emotion could well be your internal guidance system trying to prod you in the direction that is right for you.

Creative Thinking

Creative thinking is an important part of your continuing progress. This is not to say that you have to turn into a Picasso or even an Andy Warhol. Creative thinking means using your imagination a little to provide you with clues as to the best possible outcome of certain actions.

Once again at the risk of stating the obvious, thoughts that give you strong positive feelings are likely to contain some elements of truth which are worth taking seriously. Conversely, thoughts that create strong negative emotions are probably not in your best interests to pursue. Yes we know how absurdly self-evident this may sound, but ask yourself honestly how often in your life do you blindly pursue a course of action whilst ignoring the voice of your emotions?

A DIFFICULT DECISION MADE EASY

Trudy had been suffering from a serious illness, but had started to make good progress using a combination of orthodox and holistic treatments and techniques. Now that she was making progress, her mind was beginning to think of those things that she

would do with her life again. She was a full-time mother of three young children.

Having been very successful in publishing, it was little surprise when her old company invited her back to work. In various coaching sessions prior to this, she had made it very clear that returning to work in her old capacity was not an option she wished to consider. However, once the offer had been made, she then found herself being drawn back into the old thoughts and temptations. The prospect of some extra cash and intellectual stimulation would probably balance out the commuting and the pressure, she reasoned.

Before long this possibility had become a vexing question. Having absorbed much information on the mind/body connection she was aware of the fact that stress had probably brought some of her dis-ease into her life. Yet despite all that she now knew she was seriously considering this invitation back to work.

In the end Trudy discussed this problem with us. The first question we asked her was "where does going back to work come on your wants list?" She didn't even need to look at her wants list. She knew going back to work was not on it. She realised straightaway, just by answering this simple question that her feelings were guiding her right away from a return to work. She had been unaware of this fact because she had only been consulting her head – her intellect – instead of asking herself how she felt emotionally. She turned down the offer, focused her attention back onto her family life and her own health and continued to enjoy the new happiness that her healing had brought about.

Can You Have What You Want?

Often, the reason that we ignore the inner voice is that we do not believe that we can have, or deserve to have, what we want. Instead we do what we think others want us to, or settle for some unsatisfactory compromise. Yet it may be that anything you want or at least some aspect of it is within your reach, however unlikely it may seem at this moment. Perhaps you prevent yourself from focusing on your true desires simply because you believe them to be impossible and you therefore ignore your feelings and emotions about those unfulfilled wants.

If you've made a lifetime's habit out of denying

your own feelings and desires it can take a lot of courage to start admitting to 'your truth'. But if you practise these techniques (meditation, wants lists, working with Universal Laws) you can apply them to health, wealth, relationships or any area of your life. The more you understand yourself the more you'll be able to sustain the improvements you have started to make. But to hope that you can lead a totally happy and healthy life without using the best guidance of all, the guidance given through your emotions, is like trying to win Wimbledon without a tennis racket.

Releasing Buried Trauma

As you start to pay attention to your emotions and thus become more aware of those things that make you feel good, you may also start to be aware of other situations that you need to address. For example many of us have blocked out unpleasant memories because we know of no other way of dealing with the events involved. Some of us may even have been too young to remember sad and traumatic events and yet we may still feel that something is lurking in our memory that has caused us to adopt some negative outlook on life ever since and from which dis-ease may have sprung.

As you continue your improvements you might become aware that this event (or events) is something that you want to address or find out more about. On the other hand you may also feel scared by it as you fear the effects that resurrecting it may have on your life as it is now. You can find yourself locked in a battle between wanting to know the truth – and possibly finding the real cause of a long-standing condition – and wanting to stay in ignorance, thus avoiding any scary confrontation.

A Learning Opportunity

In Chapter 6 we spoke about the pain that can be experienced in making changes. We would suggest that this pain is always outweighed by the benefits that you experience when you start to work with your inner wisdom and guidance. It is possible that the traumatic event in the past happened to you for a reason, in the same way as illness may happen to you for a reason; it very possibly contains a lesson from which you are meant to learn. The negative feelings that you may have about it are likely to be as much to do with your fear of not being able to cope with the memory of the situation as with the event itself. The best way of overcoming that fear is to try to understand the lesson that you can learn through the experience that you have had.

So what on earth can events, which seem to have no positive aspects, teach us?

It is stated by some philosophers that we are all healers, teachers and/or creators. It could be therefore that every experience we have is in order that we can use our own inborn talents to convert that experience into something positive that will help us to grow as an individual and enable us to help others to do the same. Whether we go on to heal someone, teach someone, or create something out of that experience, is up to us as individuals. If we ignore it, we will often find that similar experiences occur throughout our life that will continue to give us the opportunity to teach, heal or create.

Helping Others

These events can give you, for example, an understanding of how other people may feel who have gone or are going through similar 'sufferings', in order that you may pass on your knowledge and experience. Suddenly, something that has seemed like a burden all your life can become a positive opportunity as you find yourself now able to help someone else who is going through something of a similar nature. Both parties, be they the person who is currently experiencing pain or the one who has in the past, benefit as they discuss their emotions and thoughts. New meaning is given to an experience that may have once seemed pointless and cruel.

TRANSCENDING VICTIMHOOD

Frances had been abused by her grandfather when she was young. Like so many victims of abuse it had left her feeling guilt-ridden, dirty and angry.

In her late twenties she was diagnosed with a pre-cancerous condition of the cervix and immediately started medical treatment. The hospital experience shocked her so much that she sought out complementary approaches. She was treated with homeopathy and Reiki (energy healing) and she learned how to meditate.

Frances chose to dispense with her medical treatment as she became more and more confident of her own involvement in her healing. However she did return to the hospital to be tested some months later and was found to be completely clear. This gave her new encouragement and she decided to learn techniques of energy healing herself. Then she began to practise her new found skills on friends and family.

After some months she found herself helping many people. One case in particular stands out in her memory; that of another young woman who had experienced childhood abuse. This woman felt able to share her story with Frances, as it was the first time she had met another person who had gone through something similar. Frances's traumatic experience had now turned itself into a precious gift as she helped someone else come to terms with locked up feelings of anger and shame.

Frances said she had had no idea that her own suffering could end up helping other people in such a way.

So how do we discover whether a condition of physical, mental or emotional suffering has been triggered by an event from a much earlier stage of your life? Do you need to submit yourself to psychotherapy, hypnotic regression or counselling?

Not necessarily, though all of these have their place. But if you follow your own truths you may find that whatever information you need to know will be given to you through your emotions in the present moment.

As you learn to still your active mind more regularly and thus activate this powerful healing ability, trapped negative energy is released in the most painless way that your inner intelligence can manage – sometimes bypassing the conscious mind altogether.

This might be through dreams that you may not even remember having; sometimes it may be through a discharge connected to an infection; it may be through an intense fit of tears or even laughter. Whatever way it comes out, you can trust that there is no easier or more painless way of releasing it.

A New Attitude To Past Events

When these negative energies do start to get released, it is the proof that you have begun to learn the lessons that you need to learn. You are making the changes in your life that are necessary to lead a peaceful life and you are letting your intuition guide you in whatever direction seems right. Learning a lesson from a past experience does not mean getting stuck in the past by going back to that particular time and learning now how you should have dealt with it then. The only time that is important is the present. So if you are doing the things that are best for you now, if you are undoing the things that upset you now, you have by definition learnt what you were meant to learn.

With this understanding you can proceed in the knowledge that there is nothing in your past experiences that you have any need to fear now. It is important to understand that it is no longer the event that fuels your dis-ease, it is your fear. If you can accept that all the time it was only an opportunity to learn, the fear dissolves and when the fear dissolves there may be nothing left to feed the flames of this particular dis-ease.

Joyful Perception Of The World

Once you've started to make the changes necessary to create a happier, healthier life, you'll find that the cumulative positive effects are irresistible. The desire to learn more about yourself increases, as does the desire to help other people understand how they can help themselves. As you start to introduce other people to inspirational stories, the tools of meditation, holistic therapies and informative books, so you will find that your own well-being goes from strength to strength. You are no longer living in the grip of fear; you are living a life full of optimism where you'll discover how much you have to enjoy and to offer others.

Checklist

1 Self-knowledge becomes of critical importance as you learn to use the guidance of your emotions; you must know what you want and how you feel, not just what you think intellectually.

2 Practice the affirmations "I can have what I want" and "I deserve to have what I want".

3 Past events, however traumatic, always present an opportunity to learn...and to teach, heal or create.

4 Your inner wisdom will allow you to release and heal trapped negativity from upsetting experiences in the most painless and natural way possible.

137

5 Congratulate yourself – you are beginning to find out how to live joyfully in the present moment.

8

Coping With Setbacks

"Self-acceptance comes from meeting life's challenges vigorously. Don't numb yourself to your trials and difficulties, nor build mental walls to exclude pain from your life. You will find peace not by trying to escape your problems, but by confronting them courageously."

J Donald Walters
(Romanian author, lecturer and composer)

Whether your dis-ease has manifested itself as a serious physical illness, depression or a common cold, there will be times when you feel unable to cope with the debilitating effects of the symptoms.

Fear And Confusion

It is now that, in many ways, you face the ultimate test of your new approach to your well-being. When you're lying in bed completely exhausted and drained from the physical effects of illness and scared about what the next few hours or days will bring, it's hard (to say the least) to remember all the ideas that you may have found inspirational up to now. At times like these you may try to focus on the right thing, only to find that your mind is unhelpfully awash with an array of disjointed ideas. For those who reach this position, we hope this chapter in particular will be worth revisiting.

The first thing to remember is that frequent or even continuous meditation at these times can bring dramatic improvements and reduction in pain and fear.

Two Key Concepts

Apart from meditation, there are two simple ideas worth applying whenever fear and suffering seem to be taking hold. We don't want to overload you with information at a difficult time, so these concepts are explained as briefly as possible below. We believe that an understanding of their importance will enable you to regain control of your thoughts, which in turn may enable you to take back the responsibility that we are all too willing to give away when our defences are weakened.

Please also remember to take the pressure off yourself at this point by relaxing your attachment to finding a cure. Your goal during suffering is always primarily to achieve peace of mind. Become at peace and anything is possible.

Acceptance

When you're struggling with your condition, you need to have a thought that is very simple and that also enables you to keep control of the situation. The thought of acceptance does just this. Just as we have described why it is so important to accept exactly where you are now in life, so it is just as important to accept every twist and turn of your physical or mental symptoms, however distressing they may seem.

When suffering an onslaught of unpleasant symptoms, it is possible that the mental fight that you put up against them causes you to feel more tired, more depressed and more scared than you otherwise might.

141

By fully accepting your physical state/external circumstances at any time you are avoiding the mental fight; when you manage to avoid the mental fight, your internal medicines and painkillers are better placed to enable the illness/emotional distress to pass as quickly as possible through your system. Peace of mind becomes a very real possibility whereas fighting the condition only causes those particular symptoms to become more agitated, to move more slowly and to reduce your own ability to cope.

By accepting these symptoms, you're reducing the negative effects of any dis-ease in your system and distress in your life. You are also accepting responsibility and by accepting responsibility you are taking control. When you take control you can go only in the direction that you want to – that of the relief of suffering.

BARRY TELLS GILLIAN'S STORY

Gillian came to me suffering from acute cystitis. Two rounds of antibiotics had failed to shift the condition and her doctor had told her that a hospital examination would be necessary if it didn't clear up in the immediate future.

She thought she had come to me for a 'cure'. I informed her that we don't do cures, we leave that to the client! I suggested that peace of mind was the first step to aim for, because if she was at peace she couldn't be suffering. The way to peace of mind is through awareness and acceptance.

To help her achieve this she was asked to shut her eyes and was then asked to do a simple relaxation exercise which involved her focusing her attention on each part of her body starting with her right thumb, second finger of the right hand etc (the body scan meditation). I asked her to be aware of any feelings of discomfort/pain in each part and to acknowledge it (without trying to fix it or push it away) before moving on to the next body part.

Ten minutes later we had gone round the whole body; she had barely noticed any feelings of discomfort other than a sensation of nervousness in her stomach which she put down to coming over and meeting me for the first time. Other than that, for the first time in two weeks, her body was not sending out any worrying messages.

She was asked a few seconds later how her body felt, and then again and again. The same reaction came – generally she felt at peace. I suggested to her that there was no reason why she shouldn't go on from present moment to present moment experiencing the same feeling of peace. This was the ideal place from which to begin her 'cure'. She left in a much more relaxed frame of mind, realising that her body was not like a runaway train on the way to destruction after all. Her cystitis cleared up without further intervention.

Trust

The word 'trust' links closely to acceptance. Once you've decided to accept what is happening to you, the next thing you have to do is believe that it is happening to you for a good reason (yes we know this is easier said than done).

Everything we've said in this book so far has been leading you to a greater understanding of how you really function. We hope you've started to see examples of your inner guidance system at work and are now beginning to realise that there really is something there to guide you whenever you need help. Now, when you least feel you have any reason to do so, is the very time that you most need to trust.

By taking responsibility for yourself, meditating regularly and reading books that inspire you, you've come a long way towards healing yourself. Not even the worst physical setbacks can move you backwards now even though it might seem that way sometimes. But by trusting entirely what is going on in your body/life you're placing faith in your inner wisdom to guide you in a way that is in your best interests.

Sometimes you may feel guided to visit the doctor – even if it's only to get some reassurance; sometimes you may be guided to cancel a holiday that was hindering your recovery because you were worrying so much about not being able to go on it; sometimes you may be guided to stay in bed and rest for a whole week/month/year while your body recovers.

Whatever guidance you receive through your emotions, the point is that you can trust that guidance implicitly. The more you tell yourself that you trust what is going on, the clearer that guidance will become.

Repetition of the affirmation that follows may help you to cope with the very worst of setbacks:

"I accept and trust everything that is happening to me." An even smaller step if you don't feel you can accept or trust yet, would be to repeat this line: "I accept that I have a problem with everything that is happening to me". This sentence maybe something you are better able to feel and will still take you into the world of acceptance. There is no point in affirming something that does not feel real, so if that first sentence leaves an empty or hollow feeling, try the second and start from there.

If a shorter mantra is easier, repetition of either the word 'trust' or 'thank you' can produce similar results. It may seem perverse to focus on one's own suffering and then thank it – but experience has shown us that it really does work like magic. It forces you to drop the fight. In fact eleven years of coaching clients through various types of dis-ease has confirmed to us both that 'thank you' is probably the greatest non-invasive painkiller in the world.

KATHY

Kathy had suffered from a congenital heart defect from birth. She was in her thirties, married with a young son, when she was admitted as an emergency to hospital suffering with acute pneumonia.

She was placed in intensive care and her

condition deteriorated further as she suffered a series of cardiac arrests and lapsed into a coma. In her periods of consciousness she made it quite clear (through writing) that she felt she was going to live. That she wanted hope and patience for company, not panic and despair.

Consequently she was read stories and case histories that contained messages of hope. She repeatedly focused on the need to accept her physical state in the present moment. She was given energy healing and in our sessions we asked her to imagine and trust that her body was like a winter garden; above ground it looked dead, lifeless, but beneath the surface the roots were working away helping to create a body that would bounce back to life in 'spring'. This analogy helped her to accept and trust in whatever process was going on.

Against all expectations Kathy survived a very serious heart operation. Her life appeared to hang in the balance for many weeks but very gradually she started to regain her strength. After seven months in intensive care she proved the winter garden theory to be correct and was discharged from hospital. She still had physical problems, but Kathy demonstrated that sometimes the best thing we can do is to trust what is going on – even if we don't understand the reasons why something may be happening.

The first day she walked with her son into school following her long hospitalisation, she was cheered up the steps to the building. She has since written her own book of her experience and all she learned from it; a story that has already gone on to help and inspire others.

Checklist

1 Acceptance means drop the fight! Fighting wastes energy so stop beating yourself up. Taking responsibility for your circumstances does not mean blaming yourself.

2 Acceptance also means acknowledging your truths. Don't try to sweep pain or fear under the carpet, identify areas that worry you and work on accepting their existence.

3 Trust becomes ever more important, the more fear tries to overwhelm you. Keep affirming your trust in your own power to heal.

4 Is there a reason for distressing symptoms? Remember that all setbacks may contain an important message and their pain or discomforts are a wake-up call to ever-greater consciousness.

5 Use the smallest of small steps to get you into the world of acceptance. "I accept that I have a problem with…" is a powerful affirmation to get you into the world of acceptance and out of fear.

9

Our Children

"Attitudes are transmitted to our children daily via our unconscious."

Dr Andrew Stanway,
Preparing For Life

You might now be thinking that the ideas in this book are all very well but that they cannot be applied to a child – after all, how can you explain to a four-year old the meaning of responsibility?

You might even think that you can start applying the theories of self-healing to yourself but that your children will have to rely on outside help until they are old enough to start thinking for themselves. You might imagine that it's only when they are mature enough to make their own decisions that they will be able to understand a holistic approach to health and life.

But consider this. Every day even the smallest babies are making decisions for themselves about their immediate needs and wants – not with their as yet undeveloped intellects but with their own inner wisdom.

Even Babies Can Communicate

If a baby is in real distress, it is usually successful in communicating this fact to its carers. If a toddler is in pain or suffering dis-ease of any sort, again there will be signs that almost anyone can recognise. So it goes on through childhood, adolescence and into adulthood. Every one of us is fully able to recognise when something in life is out of balance.

If you are a parent and can accept that this recognition of pain, illness or dis-ease is a straightforward ability that we all have, it could enable you to start thinking of your children, however young, in a less fearful way.

Knowing that any child can communicate with you to let you know when something is badly wrong is a major step toward understanding how responsibility can relate to your children. The way they communicate imbalances might be for example through crying, appetite loss, anger or displaying listlessness.

Importance Of Parents' Attitude

Parents then have to decide what course of action will be best for their child and what treatment, if any, needs to be sought. Perhaps the most important aspect of your behaviour at such a moment is to be conscious of your own mental approach toward their illness. Children of all ages are extremely sensitive to your thoughts and can be deeply affected by your fears.

It's been suggested in this book that we have all been brought up to fear illness. There's no blame to attach to anyone for this; it's just been a fact of life for many centuries. But as you carry out the ideas that we have suggested and begin to realise that each illness may have a reason, you've started to ease the burden of fear on yourself from each illness that you may get. Exactly the same rules can be applied to your children.

Just as with adults, it is possible that every child gets an illness for a reason. It can be an opportunity for both child and parent to learn.

153

For example, a child may get an illness in order that its immune system can become stronger thus enabling it to fight off more dangerous viruses that may try to invade in the future. We see this working with a virus such as chickenpox, which most of us get during childhood and which is generally not too serious. We suggest that childhood diseases both strengthen the growing immune system and arrive early in our lives in order to avoid an attack in adulthood, when the suffering caused can be much greater. For a healthy child it is usually sufficient for the parents to give love and basic nursing care, whilst allowing the child's immune system to deal with the virus.

Another reason a child may get an infection or illness is in order to expel any toxins that its body may be housing. The source of these toxins may have been drugs such as antibiotics or vaccines, or environmental pollution. Because their energy bodies have not suffered as many attacks as the average adult's, children usually have much less baggage to deal with before reaching the cause of dis-ease. The efficiency of their bodies' action can be very fast. That may be why it is not unusual for a child to manifest a second illness soon after having drugs for an initially different symptom. It is possible that the chemicals have suppressed the first symptom and the body must find another way of correcting that initial imbalance as well as trying to rid itself of the chemicals as quickly as possible before they cause too much damage.

REBECCA'S EAR

Rebecca was three years old. After a very traumatic birth, she had always enjoyed very good health apart from the usual minor coughs and colds. One day her parents noticed a little matter discharging from her right ear.

She was given holistic treatment, in this case homeopathy. Her parents monitored her general state of mind regularly, ensuring that they did not show their distress at what was before long, an unpleasant-smelling, copious discharge steadily emitting from her ear. Rebecca's state of mind was absolutely serene – she did not appear even to notice this discharge.

Four days elapsed during which the ear continued to discharge and Rebecca behaved absolutely normally, oblivious to the ear. She continued receiving homeopathy throughout.

Several more days elapsed before the discharge stopped smelling and became clearer in colour. A few more days after that it finally began to dry up. The condition lasted for a total of nearly two weeks, during which a large quantity of material had been emitted from her ear.

At no stage throughout this period was Rebecca feverish, in pain or in any way suffering distress. She had a good appetite and played and slept normally. The parents made a special effort to show no worry or fear. This relaxed environment was certainly crucial to Rebecca's continued peace of mind and lack of fear, which in turn may have enabled her to self-heal successfully.

Drugs would almost certainly have halted the discharge, but it is equally possible that the condition was caused by a build up of internal toxins that needed to be released. Rebecca's hearing, ears and general health have all been excellent from that time until the present (a period of ten years).

Listening Skills Needed

To consider that this self-healing process is going on inside every single child, just as it is (as long as we don't sabotage it) in every single adult, is to give us and our children a great deal of faith in our own ability to recover from illness. To give our children this faith, which we can do by finding out how they really feel – that is by listening to them – is to start them on the right path of taking responsibility in life for their own well-being. Our careful attention and listening enables them to express their true state and feelings. This empowers them with a sense of responsibility that can stay with them throughout life.

Validation Is A Powerful Tool

Being a parent is not all about 'fixing' our children's woes. Sometimes the most powerful and healing exchange a parent can have is when they are just able to hear their child's complaints without feeling they need to sort them out. For instance a child that is crying because they have just cut themselves or banged their knee will benefit far more from the parent who comforts them and acknowledges their pain ("that must hurt") than from the parent who fails to acknowledge their pain ("stop crying, it's nothing").

Just as adults sometimes want to be able to share frustrations, worries or pains with people without having them offer numerous solutions, so children too sometimes just want someone who will hear them.

JAKE

Jake was 16 years old and causing major problems at home and at school with his anger and anti-social behaviour. This had resulted in suspension from school and grounding at home – neither of which seemed to be helping him to change his ways. He was becoming a heavy user of marijuana and alcohol as well.

In our first visit he was asked what he would do with his life if time, money, health, education were no object. The answer came back immediately. "Music" – he replied. He had a passion for playing the electric guitar.

We pursued this topic further. Jake was desperate to learn more about recording and the music business and was totally bored by his present education.

We then met with his parents to explain our impression of Jake's situation. He was being forced to go into an environment every day that he hated, to learn things he no longer cared about and with which he felt no connection. Was it any surprise he was behaving angrily? We encouraged his parents to engage in a real discussion with him about the practicalities and implications of leaving his present school and finding a music based education. We asked them not to try to 'fix' his problems, but at least to start by acknowledging them.

In this discussion (at which we were not present) Jake's parents found a different young man coming through. He was animated, excited and eloquent as he told them about his musical desires. They engaged with him and whilst they were very challenged by the idea of him pursuing a career in music, they were impressed by how mature he suddenly appeared.

Jake's anti-social behaviour started to change immediately. And it wasn't short-lived – it continued and is continuing still. Within 6 months he had left school having managed to secure a place at a leading UK music & sound recording college. He excelled in

this environment and qualified as the leading guitarist from his year.

Projection

The biggest problem that many of our children may have is not their own view of dis-ease, but the view of dis-ease that we project onto them. Such projection can affect children from the age of one day to young adulthood. We tend to project our own fears of illness and of our inability to cope; being young and easily influenced, they pick up on this fear and immediately find themselves unable to cope. After all, sensing that our parents are worried on our behalf can be disconcerting enough for an adult; for a child it might mean the difference between creating health and creating ill health.

A Common Scenario

Let's imagine a first-time mother who, though she may instinctively know that there is nothing seriously wrong with her baby, starts to become worried by the fact that the thermometer has indicated a fever. At this stage the baby may be showing little sign of discomfort. The father comes home and on hearing that his child has a fever, promptly takes the temperature again himself, gets the same reading and also starts to worry.

This anxiety builds over the next hour as the temperature, which is measured often, shows no sign of coming down. The parents talk about this worrying condition in the baby's room, and the baby starts to react to the fear in their voices. Soon the baby becomes anxious as a direct result of the parents' concern. The baby starts to cry and the parents get even more upset. The baby's cries turn to screams. The parents rush the infant out into the cold night for an emergency appointment at the surgery, all the time showing signs of fear that only increase the child's distress.

By the time they reach the doctor's surgery they are all in a highly stressed state. The doctor takes one look at the child and recommends a dose of paracetamol and a good night's sleep. As the mother's own instinct told her at the start, there was never anything seriously wrong. The parents immediately start to relax, the baby responds to their changed mood and stops crying. They all return home having gone through an alarming set of circumstances that, had the parents really paid attention to the baby's state of mind instead of to the thermometer, need never have happened.

Children Deserve Respect

The authors believe that there is a tendency in our society to treat children with far less respect than they deserve. Children must be listened to. They hold the key to their own health and only need to be guided by us in the right direction for them to benefit from all the power that we have talked about in this book.

As your own self-knowledge and trust grows, so your confidence grows in your ability to give your children exactly what they need just when they need it. Whether they need to be left alone for a while to rest, whether they need hugs and reassurance that nothing is really wrong, whether they need to visit a holistic practitioner or an orthodox doctor, the feelings that you have as a result of their state of mind will guide you towards the appropriate action.

If visits to the doctor become necessary less often, your children will become accustomed to feeling in charge of their own bodies and their own health. If treatment seems necessary it may be worth considering visiting a holistic practitioner first, because this will enable the continuation of a natural approach. In this way the child will be dealt with in a holistic way that will remind both child and parents that every aspect of life is important in dealing with illness. The emphasis will remain on the person, not the dis-ease. When children are made aware that what they are doing, saying or feeling is going to be taken seriously, they naturally become more responsible human beings.

It is never too late for any of us to start taking responsibility; it is certainly not too late to start teaching our children how to do the same thing. The body is there to be trusted and our children can be made aware of this from the start of their lives. We do them a grave injustice if we consider that their youth makes them incapable of accepting any type of responsibility, or makes them too untrustworthy to be telling – or being told – the truth.

By teaching them now what we as adults are just beginning to learn, we can help them to attract only those things in life that they want right from the start. By enabling them to create only what they want, they automatically avoid creating the things that they do not want. Dis-ease will find it that much harder to play a part in a life full of ease.

CHLOE

Chloe was 17 yrs old and had been diagnosed depressed and suffering from Obsessive Compulsive Disorder (OCD). When we first met she weighed under 6 stone and her condition was clearly becoming extremely serious. Her mother had had to give up her job in order to monitor her at home; her weight was tested every day and her food and water intake was being watched.

Anti-depressants had been prescribed to little effect and meetings with psychiatrists had seemingly only further reinforced Chloe's belief in the seriousness of her problems.

She was asked the same question as Jake in our first meeting. If time, love, health, and money were no object what would you be doing? Her answer?

"Art".

When asked what she was currently studying, the answer came back:

"Maths, physics and chemistry".

Why? Her mother, a teacher, took up the story.

"Because she got 'A' Star at GCSE in those subjects and only an 'A' in art. And anyway, everyone knows those three subjects fit well together. They'll get her into a good university, she could do a science degree, maybe a science PhD – and then she'll be able to get a great job in a research lab or something like that".

All of which would be fine, if of course Chloe liked sciences in the first place. But she didn't. Not really. Not with a passion. The fact that she was good at them was irrelevant – we can all be good at things we don't enjoy.

A few minutes later Chloe showed us some of her artwork. It was incredibly detailed. Her passion shone through in her work. Her immediate situation and a reason for her OCD became very clear.

In being guided into doing sciences, the logic of which was easy to understand, Chloe was compromising her passion and had relinquished control of her future. What was now spreading out in front of her was a future that would involve study and a lifelong career in something that she wasn't really passionate about. It is possible that this loss of control over her life was pressurising her into looking around for anything over which she could still exert control. That thing became her body.

She became obsessed with controlling her calorie

intake; she became obsessed with drinking large volumes of water; she became obsessed with cleaning her body until it was red raw and she became obsessed with exercising until she could barely stand up.

We encouraged her parents to hand Chloe back her control in life. Knowing that the smallest steps are vital in crisis, we asked them just to live with the idea of art as being important in some way to Chloe, without doing anything about it right away. We suggested that the right action would become clear. It always does. Ask the right question, the answer always comes.

Three weeks later, unprompted, one of Chloe's tutors suggested she give up chemistry and take up art. Another couple of weeks later and Chloe got herself an occasional job in a school for handicapped children doing art with them and followed this by getting a job in a high street shoe shop on a Saturday. All this from a girl who a few weeks previously did not want to be seen out in public.

By the end of the following term, Chloe had been offered a bursary to study art in a specialist college, leaving her sciences behind. She came off her anti-depressants over a short period of time. Throughout this period her OCD symptoms gradually subsided as she started to get a real foothold in life. Her need to control things was being replaced by the freeing up of her creativity.

With her weight back to normal and a college course nearly behind her, it is fair to say that Chloe has now fully regained her appetite for life.

Checklist

1 Yes you can help your children too – and it's never too early or late to start.

2 When a child is ill or distressed the attitude of the parents can have a powerful influence on the child's experience – if you're fearless then so will they be.

3 Our culture does not encourage parents to listen to children or to treat them with respect – so let's change that culture!

4 Validate, validate, validate. Fixing every problem your child ever has, or even offering them solutions every step of the way, will create a child who is

dependent upon others for answers. Increase the amount of times you validate their experience without necessarily offering fixes.

5 You can help your child to grow up as someone who takes responsibility for his/her health and happiness right from the start.

10

Root Causes – Money
And Relationships

"These roots can be uncovered and excised only in an atmosphere of utter honesty."

M Scott Peck,
The Road Less Travelled

Our intention, as stated at the beginning of the book, has been to guide you through the natural process of tracing possible causes of dis-ease, in order that you may address those causes.

You might have imagined at the start that this would entail taking a journey backwards towards some dim and distant event, possibly traumatic, lurking in your past. Whilst past events may well have risen to your consciousness, travelling backwards is the last thing you have been doing. Your progress has been only in a forward direction.

You've gone forward into a new understanding of responsibility; you've gone forward by allowing yourself the time to get to know the 'real' you through spending time with yourself and through listening more to your emotions; you've gone forward by accepting the need to change and by recognising your real desires and wants; you've gone forward by opening your mind to the possibility that there is maybe more to illness than conventional thinking would have you believe. Every step, by the very nature of the fact that it is being taken now or will be taken in the future, can only ever be a step forward.

Past choices that you consider to have been wrong are in fact opportunities for you to progress now. This whole approach is not about pointing a finger of blame at yourself and saying "I shouldn't have done that"; it's not about thinking that you're a bad person due to your past actions or thoughts; it's about recognising that there may indeed be something misguided in your attitude or in your actions, but it is something that you can now correct.

Where To Look For Causes Of Stress

We suggested earlier in the book that dis-ease may stem from stress of some form or another. We've said it's possible that stress somehow damages our energy systems and that it's this damage that later leads to the onset of physical or mental dis-ease. When searching for the cause of dis-ease therefore, you're looking for areas of your life that may have brought, or are currently bringing, stress.

In this way you avoid the temptation to blame third-party influences for your poor health or unhappiness. By the very nature of the fact that it is your own mind or your own body that may be showing signs of illness, you can be certain that the cause for that illness is likely to lie within yourself. For some people this responsibility may continue to be too much to accept. It's much easier and much less painful to blame all sorts of outside influences for your poor state of being. The fact remains, your own dis-ease, your own unhappiness, may stem from your own unwillingness to assume complete responsibility for every aspect of your life.

The steps in this book have been mapped out to help you acquire the right sort of help and information to enable you to pursue your own individual course of healing. Assuming that you work through these ideas, meditate regularly and learn to recognise your genuine wants, then you may be getting closer to finding your own root causes. So what are these possible causes of dis-ease that have played such havoc with your body or mind?

At Home And At Work

The truth may be much less frightening than you may once have thought. Because of the steps that you have already taken you may find that many of the causes have already been dealt with, at times with effort, at other times with ease. Just by listening to yourself and changing your life, in however small a way, to bring you less stress and more enjoyment, you'll have reduced the number of possible causes of dis-ease. Of those that are left, you may not find a pollutant or a toxin amongst them. The remaining causes of dis-ease are likely to be found in the very areas in your life that are most important to you – namely those people and things with which you have close associations and which really 'push your buttons'.

If everything at home and at work is genuinely

how you want it to be as guided by your inner wisdom, then there is not only a very good chance that any old stresses will be allowed to leave you almost unnoticed, but also there will be no new opportunities for stress to cause damage.

However it is very often the case that we do not feel entirely at ease about either our personal or working life. It is because we invest so much of our time and emotion into these particular areas that any negative experiences potentially contain great power to cause damage initially in our energy bodies and eventually in our physical bodies.

So it is here where you may finally look for the roots of any problems. It is in your ability to assess with complete honesty the problems of any part of your upbringing, present relationships, daily stresses and frustrated desires that you also have the ability to remove the problems and treat the causes of dis-ease. True recognition of your wants is useful in an honest assessment of all of these areas; the daily increase of self-awareness that meditation helps to bring about can help these wants to become your reality and your dis-ease to become your past.

When these possible causes have been identified,

you will immediately begin to feel more relaxed about your state of being; just by identifying these problems, we believe you can substantially weaken their hold over you. Eradicating a cause altogether will often be a question of facing your fear in relation to that cause. You will find that, whenever you really do face your fears, your ability to overcome them is greater than you ever realised.

Money

WILLIAM

William had never found earning money a problem. He had made it a priority to accumulate wealth and had climbed his way up the ladder, achieving everything he had wanted by his late thirties. He had a wife and young children.

However, the more he worked and the more successful he became, the more he realised that he was not attaining the joy that he thought would come with a certain amount of money. He soon found himself drinking heavily and a major problem developed at home as his wife became less tolerant of his late homecomings and drunken state.

The realisation that money wasn't the answer he

had been seeking all his life came as a big surprise to William. This realisation struck him on the day he found himself walking down his high street with enough purchasing power to buy just about anything. Yet that was the day he discovered that there was nothing he really wanted. His life seemed empty and pointless. To cope with the pain of this realisation his drinking increased and his wife has now left him, taking the children with her.

Attitudes To Money

Money, or rather our fear of not having enough, is a possible root cause of dis-ease. It seems to have the power to wreck relationships, health and cause all manner of woes. We seem to think that it is a monster which is wonderful when on our side, but disastrous when working against us. We often feel quite powerless to control it due to our misguided perception of its own power, and we therefore let our whole lives be governed by the need to acquire it. In short, many of us are inclined to let it control almost all aspects of our daily lives.

And yet money by itself has no power. Without a person to respond to it, money is but an inanimate object incapable of causing one iota of trouble. Money is purely a symbol. If ten million pounds were placed on a table inside an empty room, that money would remain there completely powerless – even though you might regard it as a large sum capable of changing many peoples' lives.

It is therefore not money itself that may hold the power to cause you dis-ease but your attitude towards it. We have introduced you to the Universal Law that like attracts like. If you fear not having enough money you can be certain that, throughout your life, however much you acquire along the way, you will never feel as though you have enough. You will never have enough because you will always fear the loss of what you already have. It's this fear that is important because fear equals stress. Once the stress exists, dis-ease may well start its journey toward the manifestation of physical or mental symptoms.

Wealthy People Can Fear Money Too

It may seem absurd to suggest to someone who lives in a huge house with lots of material possessions and who has a healthy bank account that one of the reasons they are dis-eased may be because of their fear of money. It may seem absurd but it is quite often true. Acquiring considerable wealth may mean your attitude to acquiring is positive, but it does not necessarily mean that your attitude to money is positive. It is worth considering that if you fear it running out, then one day it may well do just that. If you lose that fear, it is possible that you will not only always have enough for your needs, but you may also erase a major cause of dis-ease – your fear of money.

Poverty Consciousness

This may also be true of people who suffer constantly from a lack of money. For them their fear comes true on a daily basis and it is that much harder for them to see that they might be continuing to be poor by the very nature of the fact that they expect it. To many people this suggestion might seem almost blasphemous. And yet it is entirely possible that their fear of not having enough money, which again is very often passed down from generation to generation quite unwittingly, has got them to this stage and is now being lived out on a real-life daily basis. The downward spiral is very often so advanced, that they cannot see and cannot believe that they are contributing towards it. Quite understandably, trying to think any differently is very difficult.

Yet it is in the redirection of your thoughts that the power may lie. If you continue to believe in your state of lack, then there is little chance of escaping it. On the other hand if you start looking forward to your desires coming true; if you really begin to think of money as something that is readily available for your benefit and enjoyment, then you can start to attract money into your life. When you start to attract it you are clearly putting out the right thoughts and emotions. As long as those emotions remain in the positive ("All my needs are being met...") and not in the negative ("I worry about not having enough money to pay/buy/do...") you will have no fear of money and if you have no fear of it then it cannot cause you dis-ease. Change your attitude to money and you will change the results you achieve.

THE MALE AGENDA

When Barry had completed his book about men entitled *The Male Agenda* we were faced with an interesting challenge. How would we get it out there? We had no spare funds to print it and we did

not want to go down the mainstream publishing route, wishing instead to develop our own organisation, The Art of Change.

Whilst we tried to be patient and accept not having the answer, we also visualised this book in finished form. We discussed layout ideas with designers, looked for cover shots, got permissions for quotes etc. What we tried not to do was to focus on the lack of money that would prevent us from achieving our dream.

A few weeks into this process Barry realised he had not written a chapter on fatherhood – a subject very close to his heart. He settled down and wrote the chapter over the course of the next few days. In other words he invested even more time in something that he felt sure would be realised.

The day after finishing that chapter we received a phone call from a most unlikely source, offering to fund the printing of the book. Within a few months the book was printed up and it is now widely available.

Fear Of Money Very Common

However strong your intention may be to be

completely honest with yourself, the fact is most people have a problem with their attitude to money. We like to blame money, or our lack of it, when things go wrong because it again absolves us of responsibility. We put ourselves under stress for much of our lives just because we fear not being able to create enough money through doing things that we would thoroughly enjoy and that would be stress-free. Most of us have been brought up to believe that life necessarily involves a certain amount of material possessions, a certain amount of physical and mental stress and a certain amount of luck. The thought of doing something in life that brings us great joy as well as bringing us enough money, is one that makes many people feel sceptical or even guilty.

But by acknowledging that your own happiness is a primary goal in your life, you will find that money can work for you as opposed to controlling you. When you have really worked out where your true happiness may lie, you will possibly find that the money you need to realise this will come as you need it, in the same way as your intuition comes. Taking the time to listen to yourself, taking the time to find out what really makes you feel good, is the key to correcting your attitude to money. By doing this money becomes no more than a consequence of your desire, a by-product of your positive actions; a mere tool in the process rather than a reason for doing something.

Fear Of Lack (Yet Again!)

Provided that you are working in harmony with your inner wisdom, your desire for money will never be in order that you may hurt, damage or deliberately create poverty for someone else. In addition the process of acquiring your desired amount of money can be almost effortless. The knack is to focus yourself in exactly the same way as you do in meditation to allow the abundant flow of money, and not the fear of not having it, into your life.

For example, if you become say a stockbroker solely because you want to have as much money as possible, it is not only likely that you will have a highly stressful career, but also that the rewards you earn will never entirely satisfy you. If your motivation lies in your belief in the scarcity of money and a need for security then you could be setting yourself up to bring about the thing you fear most – losing it all.

Wanting money just for its own sake, or for a negative, fear-based reason such as security is not in harmony with Universal Law. Without something to use the money for the money is useless. Security is suggested here as being fear-based because ultimately there is no such thing as security. None of us can ever know what our future holds; therefore there never can be guaranteed security.

If however you become a stockbroker because you really enjoy playing the money markets and because you really enjoy the life that a stockbroker has, then your motivation is very strong; as a result you will have little attachment to earning money and therefore little fear of losing it. This is because you'd do the job regardless of the state of your bank balance.

In these two instances the job is the same, but the end results are very different because the intentions at the beginning are very different.

But what about someone who works as a stockbroker, hates the job, but does it for the high earnings which she wants for pursuing positive things in her life – maybe a nice house, paying for her children's education, a yacht or future investment in her own company? This can work out well provided that the joy of the anticipated outcome outweighs the stress of doing a job you hate.

It's no good trying to hide from our fear of money. This fear is not only extremely common but is something from which we can learn a great lesson. It's not money itself that is one of the possible causes of dis-ease, but your perception of it. If you perceive money as being an endless supply that is freely available to everyone, you are relieving yourself of much of the guilt and fear associated with wealth. The happiness in your life doesn't depend upon the money that you create – quite the reverse. The money in your life depends upon the happiness that you create. Create a life of happiness, and you can have all the money you need to keep it that way.

LIVING WITHOUT SECURITY

Eleven years ago we (the authors) decided to 'follow our joy'. We decided to do the things that made us happy and stop doing the things that brought us stress and unhappiness. We had struggled to make ends meet for many years and yet the more we worked, the less we seemed to have – either of time or money.

At that time, we had practically no money; we were renting a small two-up-two-down house and were sending our children to the local state school.

We soon discovered that our joy, apart from our family time together, was in helping people. We never advertised and yet people found out about us. We never charged yet people donated to us. As we continued to follow our happiness, meaning we continued to do the things that made us feel good about ourselves, so the money came in 'from out of the blue' to support us.

After a while we were able to rent a larger house on the edge of the grounds of the children's private Steiner school. During their years at the school the fees and rent were met somehow (we're home-educating now, through choice, not lack of funds). After nine years in that house we have recently moved into a brand-new house in a spectacular location on the edge of the village. Throughout this time we have enjoyed a fulfilling lifestyle where we have wanted for nothing. Each time that we have wondered how and where our next month's rent would materialise, we have been given what we needed. It has been and continues to be 'miraculous'.

(Many would say lucky but you will recall what we think about 'luck'.)

We neither have nor seek long-term security. We have no idea where the money we might need in six months' time will come from. We still have to work on our fears sometimes! But we are free – we can choose to spend each day as we please – which at present means we balance our time between our clients and writing as well as spending much of our time with our children. We live life on a day-to-day basis that has already brought us a lifetime's worth of experiences that we might otherwise have missed.

Relationships

Husband, wife, boss, son, grandmother, in fact any person who is close to us has the power to turn our lives upside down emotionally from one minute to the next. Why should this be so when all we want is to continue along our way in a relaxed and happy state of mind?

The answer lies again in one word – fear. It is possible that, at an unconscious or conscious level, we fear the judgement of those closest to us more than anyone else in our lives. It may sound ridiculous to state that we fear members of our family but it is because we do that their attitude to us is capable of bringing out our strongest negative emotion. It is this emotion that may lie at the root of the majority of dis-ease. Banish our fear and maybe, just maybe, we banish dis-ease.

Looking for approval

Our fear of not being approved of by those closest to us is one of the most common fears of all.

KATE

Kate worked herself into a state of exhaustion both in her job and in keeping the house immaculate. After reflecting for some time on this, she was eventually able to acknowledge that she was doing this because she wanted to get the approval of her husband, Kev. Kate felt that she had to try to impress upon him how hard she could work to show that he wasn't the only one who was contributing. The harder she worked, the more superhuman things she achieved and the greater became her need for approval.

Kev, though he tried his best, couldn't give her

the approval she sought. No amount of approval could ever have been enough because what Kate didn't understand was that until she could fully approve of herself, anyone else's approval would count for little. Unaware of this and believing that she was somehow failing to achieve what Kev wanted, Kate started to feel guilty all the time. This was in spite of the fact that Kev couldn't have been happier with her contribution.

Kate's guilt developed into resentment. She became angry because she perceived that all her efforts were going unnoticed. This situation started to impair the happiness of their relationship and Kate's health, both physical and mental, suffered.

Because Kate did not approve of herself and because she was denying her own wants (demonstrated by the fact that she was doing what she felt she should as opposed to what she wanted), she could never gain satisfaction from the purely symbolic things that represented her life. In the same way that the person who works only for the acquisition of money can never have enough money, so neither can the person who works only for the approval of others ever have enough approval.

Most relationships, whether at work or at home, may run into trouble because of the inability of one person to express their feelings at the time to the other person. In the example just given, Kate and Kev ran into trouble because she failed to share her feelings of frustration and stressed herself out by trying to attain unachievable targets.

Being Good

If we fully understand the idea that one of the most important things in life is to be honest with ourselves, then we would find ourselves more able to cope with every relationship in which we are involved. It's only in our misinterpretation of being 'good' that our weakness in our relationships lies. We tend to think being good means impressing others and getting approval from others. In fact being good starts with being honest with ourselves about what makes us feel good.

Fear Of Being Selfish

There is a deeply rooted belief in our society that it is automatically selfish to pay attention to what makes us feel good. It is this belief that our own desires are selfish and unworthy that may prevent us from leading fulfilled and happy lives. It also discourages us from looking too closely at the aspects of life that are currently bringing us distress on the basis that we are not worthy of anything better anyway. And yet it is in these very personal aspects of our lives that we may find our major causes of dis-ease. Just by addressing honestly these very emotive aspects of life, we might help to eradicate all manner of stress.

The temptation of course is to do the opposite. When we realise that there are elements of our relationships that are not working, rather than engaging with the problem we often create distractions elsewhere. These distractions can easily become problematical themselves and may manifest for example as overworking, infidelities or addictions. This is where the cause of much suffering might be found for it is when we fail to deal with unhappiness and dissatisfaction that stress begins to take hold.

Relationship Problems Seen As Opportunities

Very few of us are able to exist without relationships; we are not meant to. It is an innate aspect of human beings to be social. Being social however does not mean being dependent upon any one or any thing else for our happiness. This is where our attitude to relationships, like our attitude to money, becomes imbalanced. And it is when the imbalance occurs that dis-ease can set in.

We were given other people in the world in order to show how capable we are of love. We were given some of our senses in order to communicate. Denying complete and honest communication with another person about an issue that we know we need to talk about is representative of our own inability to show complete love not only to them, but as importantly to ourselves.

We need to remember that, in the same way as an illness represents a possible opportunity to learn, so can a problem that occurs in a relationship. If we all looked at these problems as opportunities and not just as disasters, we would realise that it is not only fair but also imperative to give every person involved in any given situation the chance to express openly and honestly their own feelings.

BILL

Bill had been brought up by his father and stepmother after his real mother had left home when he was young. His stepmother was a very caring woman with strong views on how children should be raised and his father allowed her to take control of child-raising issues.

Bill's new mother knocked herself out to do everything within her power to 'fix' everything for Bill. She also told Bill that the music he listened to wasn't appropriate; that the sculptures he loved to create (and was very good at) were not as important as the intellectual subjects that he did such as maths and business studies as these would get him a good job in the world; and that the friends he chose were not right for him and that he could do so much better.

By the time Bill had become a young man his own sense of self had been completely distorted. All the things that should have been helping him to form and contribute to his identity had been thrown out through well-meant but over-controlling parenting.

He found himself leaving home and going to

college totally unequipped to deal with social situations because he had nothing to say for himself. The removal of his passions and joys had resulted in little more than a lifeless machine going through the motions.

Bill plunged into depression and had to leave his college. He has however now started to recognise that what he most needs to do is to rebuild his identity through acknowledging and allowing his joys to surface, even if they don't fit in with his parents' or anyone else's view of what he should like and who he should mix with.

And his stepmother, having seen how Bill had become so unable to cope with life, has acknowledged her own role in that process and has started to change herself. Change that she finds scary, but ultimately which will come as a relief because she will no longer be worrying about having to make all the right decisions for someone else.

Bill is currently finding that his inspiration is the key to his balance and the key to his strength. He is changing. He now recognises that he had been brought up in a relationship which, although well meaning, had ironically impacted severely on his ability to live his own life.

Open And Honest Communication

Using the law of non-attachment, we can listen to another's point of view without having an attachment to our own opinion having to hold sway. In this way we are able to talk about each other's worst fears; we are able to express ourselves openly and freely, facing worst case scenarios in a way that can bond together all concerned.

Our failure to have a successful relationship of any sort might come down not to the shortcomings of the other person or persons, but to our own inability to express how we are feeling when we are feeling it. If you feel that your boss is working you too hard and that you need to have extra support, running round trying to work harder while all the time resenting him will only lead to further resentment and anger. If you feel that your partner is shirking his/her fair share of the housework, not talking about it will also lead to resentment and anger. If your teenage son is failing to turn up to school and is becoming antisocial at home, not engaging him in frank and open discussion about his life is only likely to lead to further problems for child and parents alike.

As we have seen already, it is when these powerful negative emotions such as anger, resentment and guilt enter our conscious thought-process that stress is caused and then possibly dis-ease.

So why do we allow these things to happen?

Very often it is because we are so scared by the thought of someone's reaction to our true feelings, that we avoid talking about them altogether. It is yet another way that we let fear control us.

Of course, not talking about our problems does not make them go away. Ignoring them is like building a house on poor foundations. You can paper over the cracks, you can make the house look lovely on the outside and every bit as nice as any other house that you have ever seen; but give it time, and that house will soon begin to show the signs of the poor work that went on earlier. Cracks will soon appear, redecoration will become an expensive and pointless exercise and eventually the house will fall down of its own accord.

When we deny the truth to ourselves, our bodies may be very like that house. Try as we may, we eventually have to give in to the relentlessness of the negative energy that has developed as a result of our inability to be totally honest about what we really wanted in those key areas of our lives. This is why, where possible, it is important to address problems as they arise.

Holism In Relationships

This is the equivalent of the holistic health care philosophy that focuses on the idea of prevention. Seeing problems in relationships as opportunities and then talking about them with the aim of reaching a solution that is agreeable to all concerned is how we prevent stress and therefore how we may prevent dis-ease.

Recognising and accepting that a problem exists gives you great power. The damage the problem can cause is lessened by that recognition alone. By then taking full responsibility for your part in the problem and by encouraging others to do the same, you can begin to undo the most tangled knot. Problems that may have already led to dis-ease can also still be undone. It's never too late to try to create a solution, no matter how advanced the problem may seem.

195

VALERIE

Valerie was married, in her thirties and a successful businesswoman who suffered from frequent migraines, irregular periods and a bad back. She had started to look at her life in a more holistic way and began to notice patterns in her various relationships (both business and personal) that seemed to relate to her health. These patterns included her own constant desire to 'bend over backwards' to help others, without first thinking of her own needs.

Through a combination of coaching and meditation Valerie became more aware of the role she was playing in these relationships. She began to notice how much she would try to give others help even if they were not asking for it. She observed how she would offer opinions when no opinion was being requested. She also noticed how she would come away from certain meetings, with her family in particular, feeling completely drained.

And so Valerie started to practise non-attachment. She began to listen to her family, friends and colleagues as they complained about their lives and, instead of trying to 'fix' their problems (all of which would have been 'unfixable' by an outsider anyway) she found herself just giving them her compassion. She listened, she paid full attention, and she tried to resist offering help and advice unless she was actually being asked for it.

She soon found herself coming away from meetings feeling energised as opposed to drained. She noticed her back, which may previously have reflected her attempts to 'support' all these people, was now giving her less pain. Her migraines became less frequent and her periods more regular.

It seemed that, as Valerie started to create a balance in her daily relationships, so her body began to reflect that sense of balance. She is now fully aware of the need to practise non-judgement and non-attachment in her relationships, a need that has been clarified by the physical improvements she has experienced.

Realising that the causes of dis-ease may lie in your attitude to those subjects that are closest to your heart, could give you the power to achieve peace of mind even in the midst of great physical suffering. The more honest you are with yourself, the more effective you can become in overcoming these unwanted

197

circumstances. Supported by a powerful technique such as meditation, you will find that each day can bring renewed peace of mind and strength. Your desire to take complete responsibility, combined with the recognition of your fears and desires, will establish a strong foundation from which to build.

Checklist

1 How much do you let your fear of not having enough money influence your decision-making? Start viewing money as a tool for your use and not an end in itself.

2 Don't put off your happiness until some imagined future (when I retire, get married, make a million pounds etc) but start to pursue what makes you feel good right now.

3 Becoming more honest and authentic with yourself will enable all the relationships in your life to become more fulfilling. Disapprove of yourself and you'll find others will always find fault in you. Start looking to accept who you are and you'll discover others will start accepting you too.

4 Well-meaning friends, family, colleagues can disempower you if you let them project their fears into your life. Don't be tempted to step into somebody else's story – hear them and listen to them but remember who you are and what your truth is. Honour your individuality – it's what makes you unique.

11

Conclusion

"If you would indeed behold the spirit of death, open
your heart wide unto the body of life.
For life and death are one,
even as the river and the sea are one."

Kahlil Gibran,
The Prophet

"No great ascent was ever made without faults and falls,
and they must be regarded as experiences which will help us
to stumble less in the future. No thoughts of past errors
must ever depress us; they are over and finished, and the
knowledge thus gained will help us to avoid a repetition of
them... All fear must be cast out;"

Not our own words, but the words of a book that
was published over 60 years ago and that has been

reprinted more than 25 times since the war. The writer, Dr Edward Bach, was aware then of what millions of us today are still unaware; that the power to cure all dis-ease might come not from without but from within.

We have tried to explain throughout this book how this knowledge can be used to try to reach a state of peace of mind and improved health. But we are aware that for some people a complete physical cure is out of the question. What help then can this knowledge be to such people?

We would answer that it can be of great help and comfort. Sometimes the greatest help one human being can offer another who is suffering, is the restoration of their peace of mind. Sometimes we can help relieve pain, although we may not be able to help restore complete physical health. These things alone are very often the difference between someone dying in peace and someone who dies racked with pain and anxiety.

JOANNA

Joanna was terminally ill with cancer. She had been in a leading cancer hospital for many months, but her consultants had finally decided there was

nothing more they could do. They made their decision to stop medical treatment. Instead of telling her themselves they had the information passed onto Joanna a few days later by a junior member of staff.

Joanna felt desperately upset at the manner in which this news was broken to her. She felt that she was being spurned by the very doctors who had, for so long, been in constant daily contact with her.

In our sessions with Joanna, she worked through her anger and fear and came to a decision. She decided to move to a hospice that would give her palliative care for her remaining days. As soon as she moved her emotional state improved. She was now in an institution served by people whose job was to help someone die in peace. Joanna immediately responded to this change in approach and felt more relaxed, calmer and more confident of what was ahead of her. Having spent much of the last few weeks prostrate in hospital with wires and tubes everywhere and drugs being constantly pumped into her body, she was now free to sit up in her room, be pushed around in a wheel-chair and take stock of her situation with a clearer mind.

When she did die she had clearly reached a deepened state of acceptance – one that is often referred to as a state of grace. It was as if she was no longer struggling to achieve an unreachable goal. She passed away very peacefully.

The subject of death is too vast and profound to explore in-depth within this book. But the important message that we would like to put forward at this point is that it is not necessarily in the prevention of death that healing can only be shown to be successful. Its success can equally be in the manner in which someone is allowed to die and this in itself can seem quite often to be 'miraculous'.

Non-Attachment To Outcome

Again this is where the practice of non-attachment is so important. If we proceed on the basis that we must at all costs help someone to recover physically, then we may find ourselves disappointed and unable to help. Our attachment to a specific outcome is creating a fear within us that the result we so desperately want may not be reached. This fear can be a major hindrance in someone's recovery, or indeed in their being allowed to die in peace and serenity.

If however we learn to accept totally every stage of life, every development of an illness however strange or worrying it may seem, we will be creating no battle and therefore no energy can be wasted. In this way we direct all our valuable resources towards improved health, be it our own or someone else's health, and we waste none of our energy on fighting fear.

For those who are going through any form of illness, however serious, we would recommend keeping this book beside the bed and re-reading it whenever you become demoralised and feel unable to cope. For we believe that in each and every one of us lie those abilities of which we have talked; the ability to ask for help, the ability to hear our inner guidance and the ability to bring about our own state of peace, our own healing.

Reminding Yourself Of The Basics

In times of crisis we need to remind ourselves of the basic rules – the direction of thoughts, listening to emotions, acceptance of symptoms. We are all relative beginners in this realisation of our own internal powers, and so if you forget occasionally be gentle with yourself. It's far more important to acknowledge your temporary slip and to try to get back on track again by reminding yourself of the new tools and information that you now have available.

Whatever our state of health, calling on family, friends, doctors, healers or therapists does not mean we are weak and failing in our efforts towards self-healing. Sometimes the extra 'leg-up' that any one of these people can offer is just the impetus we need to start believing in ourselves again. Taking an antibiotic does not mean you have failed, provided you do not assume that it has removed the cause of dis-ease. Having surgery does not mean you have failed, provided you do not assume that it has provided all of the answers. Seeing a counsellor does not mean you have failed, provided you do not assume that by simply talking about your problems you have necessarily removed them from your life.

Responsibility – Your Choice

No one else can take responsibility on your behalf for your own well-being. The only person who can do that is you. You either assume total responsibility for yourself, or you don't. The choice is yours.

If you do take charge of your own life, the simple application of all that we have written about can help to bring about substantial improvements. Once you have fully grasped the meaning of responsibility you will begin to realise the importance of complete honesty with yourself and with others. This ability to be completely honest is in itself a most powerful healing tool, and gives a feeling of self-worth and value on a daily basis.

Being honest with others about how you feel is a fundamental part of life that many consider to be of no real importance. By being honest with yourself to begin with you will find that honesty with others becomes much easier, and decisions that would previously have been awkward become effortless. Because you now know what you want and know that you do not want it in order to hurt anyone else, you'll find the strength and commitment to help your resolve. At this stage, blocks in your life and personality can start to remove themselves and doors of opportunity open all around you.

Becoming A Conscious Creator

Meditation, recognition of your true wants and a greater understanding of how powerful you really are, will help you to achieve a state of increased self-honesty. As you begin to change, you might become aware of the weight lifting from your shoulders. Not only can you feel lighter, you'll seem to move more easily through life, both mentally and physically.

By coming to terms with what is in your best interests to have and then by seeking to achieve those things, you are dropping the fight against those things that have already entered your life, but that you did not want. Instead of being in a negative state of mind you are now in the mode of positive creation. By continuing to focus on those positive aspects you will find that negativity will gradually, or suddenly, disappear.

ANDY

Andy had experienced much pain in his life. In his mid thirties when we first met he had lost both his parents (one to suicide), had a couple of siblings on anti-depressants, had separated from his wife with whom he had two children and was struggling with a job which was putting him under intense daily pressure.

He had reached a stage where he just did not know which way to turn.

In our first session he was asked to describe what he would have done if he had just spent 'the perfect three months'. We asked "Andy, three months have just gone past and they have been perfect – what have you done?"

His response to this question became the springboard for a whole new approach to life. One simple question. At first Andy's answer was quite conservative – in fact at first he couldn't even imagine anything good at all. But after he was asked a couple of questions ("have you had a holiday?", "are you now in a loving and respectful relationship?", "have you secured a big contract at work?") – he soon got the idea and the room was filled with positive and at times outrageously euphoric thoughts.

Andy wrote this perfect three months down after our meeting. He used it as a point of daily focus and he often added in more details as they came to him. Interestingly Andy started to find that some of those ideas he had described began to materialise, at times with much less effort than he would have anticipated.

This gave him the confidence to allow himself to think more often about what he wanted from life. As his confidence grew so did the results. He started to counsel his siblings, helping them through difficult times and became the rock in the family. He left his job and set up his own successful consultancy where the only boss he has to answer to is himself. Then he found a partner who he feels brings out the best in him and with whom he has now set up a new home.

Three years after our initial meeting Andy has changed his worldview and his life has changed. He stopped focusing on what was wrong in the present and what had gone wrong in the past, and changed the emphasis to focusing on what was good and what could be great. The results have reflected that change in attitude.

We believe that the power to create what we want lies in the belief of the creator – you. By putting your mind to wanting perfect health and the perfect life, and by banishing all fear that you may not achieve it, you will find that every day can bring you nearer to that goal.

We hope that the steps mapped out in this book will be used for the process of going forward towards this goal. We know that for some people this will seem like an impossible mission, but whatever your thoughts, it is surely worth pursuing the ideas until you are absolutely certain as to whether this type of approach is workable.

Going on from this book and reading further material, with the emphasis on what attracts you rather than on what you think you should read, is part of important further development. Putting this book down, without trying the methods suggested and without seeking out further alternative information, is indicative of a continued unwillingness to take responsibility. The only reason that can exist for this choice is your fear that you may be confronted with a painful truth about who you really are.

There is nothing to be feared in facing the truth, yet there may be plenty to be lost in not facing it. The truth is real and sooner or later you may have to face it if you are to heal. By denying what you really want to do or say or have or be – in other words by denying

211

the truth – you are only putting off what will one day have to be said or done or had or been if you do not wish to risk experiencing the possible physical, mental or emotional damage that such denial may incur.

So grab the opportunity that dis-ease brings with it. Find out who you really are, engage with the pain and uncertainty without trying to fix it immediately and let your wonderful inner wisdom flow through your veins and into consciousness. At the very least you'll find peace of mind – and beyond that, well the sky is the limit…

Checklist

1 Death is a part of life – it is not a form of failure. How people are allowed to die might be of as much importance as how they lived.

2 Life can become much more enjoyable once you have educated yourself on the subject of death and dying and started to accept death as a natural and potentially positive process. If death frightens you, then start studying the huge body of evidence for survival of consciousness.

3 Non-attachment to outcome and dropping a belief in failure are vital in helping yourself or another to become at peace with serious or terminal illness.

4 Becoming a conscious, positive creator is the outcome of taking complete responsibility for every aspect of your life. Focus on the ideal solution, not on the problem.

5 It may be scary to face the truth about yourself – but it's the only way we know of to become free, joyful and at peace with yourself and the world.

About The Authors

Barry and Winnie Durdant-Hollamby have been consultants to individuals and organisations since 1996. During this time they have coached people suffering with imbalances ranging from cancer to schizophrenia, from depression to relationship crises. They have developed their own system for change, many ideas of which are included in this book. They have two daughters and live in East Sussex.

Recommended Reading

Heal Thyself by Dr Edward Bach
Quantum Healing by Deepak Chopra
Unconditional Life by Deepak Chopra
The Seven Spiritual Laws Of Success by Deepak
    Chopra
The Road Less Travelled by M. Scott Peck
On Death And Dying by Elisabeth Kubler-Ross
Teach Yourself To Meditate by Eric Harrison
You Can Heal Your Life by Louise Hay
The Continuum Concept by Jean Liedloff
Life After Life by Dr Raymond Moody
Excuse Me Your Life Is Waiting by Lynn Grabhorn
Loving What Is by Byron Katie
The Healing Path by Marc Barasch
Living In The Light by Shakti Gawain
Love, Medicine & Miracles by Dr Bernie Siegel
Eat More Raw by Steve Charter

Other books and recordings available from

The Art of Change

www.artofchange.co.uk

The Male Agenda

The world is full of men chasing that elusive something – the dream that will somehow make everything alright. Does it really exist? *The Male Agenda* challenges the reader who is struggling to make sense of life to accept compromise no longer. Creating change can be a challenging concept – even frightening. This book makes it exciting and achievable through real life stories and practical 'self help' tools.

So It's Tough Out There, Is It?

An uplifting, inspirational parable that explores the true meaning of holistic business practice. Through the medium of story-telling, this book describes how to create sustainable success in the dog-eat-dog business environment.

Stepping Stones

A tried and tested easy to follow workbook that will help you to manage transition in your life. Laid out in diary form, there are 84 steps to take which will walk you easily through your own unique journey.

Learn To Meditate In 20 Minutes

Think you can't meditate? Having trouble relaxing? Try this talked through recording, where the process of meditation becomes as simple as sticking on a CD. With gentle backing music and a technique that is used the world over by thousands of people everyday, this recording will have you feeling more relaxed within minutes.

Two Visualisations To Focus The Mind For Hospital Treatment

Audio CD – self-explanatory.

Three Visualisations To Encourage Better Health And Happiness And To Help Reduce Fear And Stress

Audio CD – self-explanatory.

Flight Of Freedom

Flight of Freedom is a nine-track music CD written and produced specifically with the purpose of enabling the listener to find an easy route to relaxation.

Bedtime Bliss

Audio CD. Over an hour's worth of gentle relaxing music to help children settle at night.

Sundown

Sundown is 78 minutes of total chill music that you're unlikely to have heard anywhere before. The music has been pooled from some of the best unsigned musical talent from around the world.

Living At The Highest Level

CD-rom. Time-management programme developed through Barry & Winnie's work.

All books and CDs created by
Barry Durdant-Hollamby.

For more details about any of the above please contact:

The Art of Change
PO Box 441
East Grinstead
West Sussex
RH18 5DH

Tel: +44 (0) 1342 823809
Email: welcome@artofchange.co.uk
www.artofchange.co.uk

For more information about coaching/consulting
please contact the above or:
www.barrydurdant-hollamby.com

Lightning Source UK Ltd.
Milton Keynes UK
UKHW010748080819
347620UK00001B/36/P